PELICAN BOOKS

Philosophy

Editor: Ted Honderich

THE RIGHT TO STRIKE

Dr Leslie Macfarlane is a Fellow and Tutor in Politics at St John's College, Oxford, and a University lecturer in Political Theory. In 1971 he was visiting Professor at Simon Frazer University, British Columbia and in 1977–8 was visiting Professor at McGill University, Montreal. His previous books include *British Politics 1918–1964* (1965), *Modern Political Theory* (1970), *Political Disobedience* (1971), *Violence and the State* (1974) and *Issues in British Politics since 1945* (1975).

L. J. MACFARLANE

The Right to Strike

PENGUIN BOOKS

Penguin Books Ltd, Harmondsworth,
Middlesex, England
Penguin Books, 625 Madison Avenue,
New York, New York 10022, U.S.A.
Penguin Books Australia Ltd, Ringwood,
Victoria, Australia
Penguin Books Canada Ltd, 2801 John Street,
Markham, Ontario, Canada L3R 1B4
Penguin Books (N.Z.) Ltd, 182–190 Wairau Road,
Auckland 10, New Zealand

First published 1981

Set, printed and bound in Great Britain by
Cox & Wyman Ltd, Reading
Set in Intertype Lectura

TO THE MEMORY OF PAUL BRODETSKY

Contents

Preface

The return to power in Britain of a Conservative Government, committed to the reform of the law relating to the closed shop and picketing, has brought accusations from union leaders of a deliberate revival of the confrontation politics of the 1971 Industrial Relations Act. Trade unions have reacted sharply to what they see as an attack on fundamental union rights, slowly and painfully built up in the face of employer and State hostility. Of all these rights the most crucial and most celebrated is the right to strike. That right has for over two hundred years been at the centre of bitter controversy in the recurrent periods of labour unrest in Britain, from the mass discontent and revolutionary fears which led to the banning of unions and strikes in 1799, to the strife-torn winters of the present.

The Right to Strike is a book about the morality, not the legality, of strike action. The questions it seeks to answer are whether a moral case can be made for workers and unions having a legal right to strike and, if so, when is its use morally justified. In the first section of the opening chapter, 'Rights and Strikes', the general nature of moral rights and the distinctive characteristics of the right to strike are analysed: in the second part the right to strike is viewed through the moral lenses of different codes and principles of social action – natural justice, Rawlsian justice, Marxism, economic individualism, Nozickian rights, and moral realism – lenses to be used in later chapters to examine the contentious and contestable nature of the right to strike.[1]

1. See W. B. Gallie, *Proceedings of the Aristotelian Society*, Vol. 56,

Chapter 2, 'Workers and Unions', seeks to bring out the historical background to the conflict and controversy which surrounds the right to strike.That right was legally established in the period of strident *laissez-faire* capitalism as the right of each individual to decide for himself whether to join a union or to go on strike; as the reciprocal of the rights of the individual employer to refuse to employ union labour, to lock out his employees and sack and replace strikers. This legal right came into blunt collision with conceptions of worker solidarity imposing moral duties to join trade unions, respond to strike calls, and resist employer attempts to give *their* jobs to 'scabs' and 'blacklegs'. The chapter concludes with a discussion of the closed shop and its impact on union claims of a moral duty to support strike action.

In the third chapter, 'The Work Process and Strikes', we turn to the part strikes actually play in the life of industrial workers in contrast to the 'role' assigned to them in the industrial relations 'process'. It is argued that the mainstream industrial pluralist approach in effect upholds the moral realist view of the right to strike as a right of the strong to enrich themselves at the expense of the weak. The chapter ends with a brief discussion of how the gradual change from economic collective bargaining to industrial democracy appears through the different moral lenses outlined above.

In Chapter 4, 'Employers and Strikes', the question is posed 'Why have employers unilaterally abandoned the lock-out and strike-breaking, while leaving unions in full possession of the pre-emptive strike?' The answer is found not so much in the increase in union power, as in the change in public and employer attitudes and the acceptance of forms of collective bargaining incompatible with employers' waging all-out industrial warfare. The present deflated employer role in strikes is critically appraised from the various moral standpoints adopted. Finally, an attempt is made to establish those situations in which a precise meaning can be given

London, 1955–56, and William E. Connolly, *The Terms of Political Discourse*, D. C. Heath, Lexington, Mass., U.S.A., 1974, Ch. 1, for a discussion of 'essentially contested concepts'.

to the notion of a 'justified strike' for employers, and to formulate moral rules for such situations.

Chapter 5, 'Workers and Strikers', is in some respects the key chapter in the book in that it seeks to establish what constitutes a binding obligation to strike for the individual workers called on to walk out on strike, to comply with a strike-meeting vote, or a union official strike call. This analysis enables firm moral conclusions to be drawn on the crucial issues of whether, and when, strikers are entitled to employ social pressure or coercion against those who do not accept an obligation to take strike action. Finally there is a full discussion of what constitutes a 'justified strike' for an industrial striker, a strike meeting and a trade union.

Chapter 6, 'Public Rights and Government Duties', examines the case for restricting the right to strike in order to protect other fundamental rights possessed by members of the community. Among the questions considered are 'Ought strikes necessarily to be banned in war time?'; 'Should members of the armed forces be allowed to join unions and take strike action?'; 'Does the right of patients to medical care take absolute priority over the right of hospital workers to strike?'; 'Are Governments entitled to use criminal sanctions against striking unions to enforce their economic policies?'; 'Are trade unions entitled to strike in protest against the Government's economic or political policies or to coerce it into changing its policies?'

The final chapter is devoted to consideration of 'The Right to Strike as a Fundamental Right' – universal, paramount and practical. It is argued that certain minimum political and trade union conditions must be met if the right to strike is to be a meaningful as distinct from a nominal right, as in the Communist States. The claim of the right to strike to be considered a fundamental human right is critically examined in the light of its characteristics as (i) a right of the employed class against the employer class, (ii) an instrumental right for the extraction of benefits for some at the expense of others, (iii) a collective right of workers overriding the rights of the individual worker, (iv) a coercive right for use not only against employers but other workers, (v) a political right

11

requiring objective conditions absent in authoritarian and totalitarian States of both the Left and the Right.

My final conclusion is that the right to strike is a keystone of modern democratic society. No society which lacks that right can claim to be democratic: any society which seeks to become democratic must secure that right.

The Polish workers, in their shipyards, mines and factories, have since demonstrated the force of these assertions. They have used the strike weapon to wrest from the weakened Communist authorities not only the right to strike and form free trade unions, but also highly significant rights of free expression. If the Polish workers are able to hold on to and consolidate the rights they have so bravely won, there is perhaps, at last, the possibility of humanizing the face of socialism. But the tyrannosaurs of the Kremlin give one grave cause for apprehension.

I dedicate this book to the memory of my dear friend and colleague, Paul Brodetsky, political theorist and industrial lawyer, whose critical appraisal and advice, so generously given in the past, would have been invaluable on this topic, so close to his interests, his principles and his deep learning. What Paul would have thought of my analysis and conclusions I shall never know, but he would, I believe, have welcomed it as a contribution to serious debate on an issue of deep and lasting concern to democratic theory and democratic practice.

Chapter 7, 'The Right to Strike as a Fundamental Right', was presented as a paper to the session on 'Fundamental Rights in a Democratic Order' at the International Political Science Association XIth World Congress in Moscow in August 1979, and part of Chapter 6 as a paper on 'Strikes against the Government' to the Easter 1980 Conference of the British Political Studies Association.

I should like to thank Ted Honderich, the editor of the Penguin Philisophy Series, for his searching criticisms of the first draft, and my wife for her encouragement and assistance throughout.

L. J. MACFARLANE

St John's College, Oxford
October 1980

One

Rights and Strikes

Rights may be seen as objective entitlements or as subjective claims. Thus the statement 'A has a right to X' may be made either as a statement of fact or as a claim. As a statement of fact the assertion will be either true or false in terms of the rules or principles governing the possession of the right concerned. In 'hard cases', however, it may be difficult to determine whether A does, or does not, have a right 'in fact' to X; A may therefore continue to allege a right 'in fact' to X in spite of a ruling to the contrary. This position has to be distinguished from a claim by A to X, where what A is asserting is not that such a right exists 'in fact', but that it *ought* to exist.

Two main categories of rights may be distinguished – legal rights and moral rights, where the latter may be expressed in terms of any set of principles or values held to be binding. Legal rights are relatively straightforward. It makes no sense for a man to claim a legal right to do what he knows he is legally prohibited from doing; although it will make sense to claim that morally he ought to have the legal right to do what the law proscribes. With moral rights the problem is more complex, since there is no one accepted moral code to which all may refer to establish their moral rights and duties. Moreover, many moral positions and values are not built into a comprehensive moral system, or lack any body authorized to determine how the principles of the system should be applied. Even where such an authority exists, as with the Pope in the realm of Catholic morality, it is still possible for that authority to be disputed by adherents. Thus it is possible for a Catholic to argue not only that he *ought* to have the moral right to practise birth-control, but that he actually *has* a right. In the former case he is disputing the way in which the Pope has exercised his rightful authority, in the latter the right of the Pope to make such a use of his authority. The assertion of a right as a Catholic to dissent from a Papal moral determination may be made positively, in that the determination may be deemed to be in direct conflict with the principles of Catholic morality, or negatively, in that it prohibits actions not morally wrong in terms of Catholicism. Where, on the other hand, no moral authority exists, or is recognized to exist within a moral system, it is not possible to talk in terms of the moral rights one *ought* to have. Since there is no body which is universally accepted as capable of withholding or granting moral rights, each person is left to assert for himself the moral rights he *has* in terms of the moral principles he recognizes.

Legal rights are of two kinds – negative and positive. Negative rights, or liberty rights, are the rights which one has to do anything not specifically required or prohibited by law, where exercising the right is not dependent on the provision of specific facilities. Included in this category are many actions not normally thought of in terms of rights (e.g. blowing one's nose), and others where the right is defined by the scope of legal prohibitions and restrictions (e.g. the legal right of free speech). Positive legal rights are rights which one would not have but for the specific provisions of the law, and which could not exist, therefore, in the absence of the law. The two categories are logically distinct; though there is a tendency for negative rights to be given a positive form in order to clarify their nature or to reinforce their status and force.[1]

Legal rights may be contrasted with legal duties. A legal right to act is always a legal liberty to act or not to act as one wishes

1. Wesley N. Hohfeld, *Fundamental Legal Conceptions*, New Haven, Conn., U.S.A., 1919; London edition (1964) edited by Walter W. Cook. Positive rights are divided by Hohfeld into claim rights against others to act in specified ways, power rights to change others' claim rights or duties, and immunity rights preventing others from imposing duties.

according to one's own determination, in contrast with the externally-imposed, sanction-backed obligation of a legal duty. The conversion of a right, such as the right to vote or the right to join a trade union, into a duty involves a loss to the individual which may be expressed as follows:[2]

1. The loss of the liberty right to determine how one will act. With the right to vote the loss operates directly only at election times; but with the right to join (and the associated right to leave) a trade union the loss is a continuous one.

2. The loss of the liberty to exercise other legal rights, through being required to fulfil the new legal duty. Compulsory voting means a loss of the right to carry out other lawful pursuits in the time I am required to use up in voting, while compulsory unionism involves a wide range of restrictions on my freedom to act as I wish within the work context. In particular I may be denied the right to belong to a non-recognized association or union which in my view would better defend my interests as an employee.

3. The direct loss of satisfaction suffered on those occasions when I am required to act contrary to my wishes. With voting this will occur if I am compelled to vote when I would otherwise have abstained, or when I am fined for non-voting. With compulsory trade union membership it will be present whenever I am aware of being a forced union member, or when I am penalized for refusing to comply.

4. The loss of the satisfaction which I would otherwise have derived from acting differently in type 3 situations – the satisfaction lost by not being able to stay at home instead of going out to vote: that lost by not being able to spend my union dues on

2. The method used here to analyse the cost of a change from right to duty was suggested by Professor C. B. Macpherson's analysis of the transfer of power from worker to employer in a market society. See his 'A Theory of Democracy' in *Democratic Theory: Essays in Retrieval*, Oxford University Press, 1973.

15

beer, or the satisfaction I would have derived from belonging to the proscribed employee association of my choice.

While the 1 and 2 losses of liberty are objective losses for all individuals concerned, the 3 and 4 losses of satisfaction are subjective – incurred only by those who would in fact have not so acted or who would have acted differently in the absence of a requirement to act. Subjectively, however, those who have no wish or inclination to act otherwise than in the ways required are unlikely to see themselves as having suffered *any* loss of liberty. They will feel free in doing what they are required to do, where that is what they want to do. Furthermore, some may see compelling reasons why others should be forced to be free – to forfeit their personal negative liberty not to do what is right, to secure the positive liberty of the collectivity of which they are a part. In such terms compulsory trade unionism appears to many ardent trade unionists as a gain in real liberty for those required to carry out their objective duty to join a trade union. Such a view, of course, itself embodies and expresses a distinctive moral attitude.

Under a legal code all members of the legal community concerned have the right to do, or to refrain from doing, anything not specifically proscribed or required by the law; as well as the right to do, or to refrain from doing, anything specifically permitted by law.

The position in morality is more complex. While a legal code has a monopoly within any polity, every moral code is faced with competitors. A moral code is thus forced to define for itself the moral situation of those persons who do not assent to its principles. In particular it finds itself faced with the question of how far the requirements of morality ought to be given legal force in one or other of the following ways:

1. Moral rights or duties which ought to be incorporated as legal rights or duties.
2. Moral duties which ought not to be legally incorporated where

the moral objection is to legal coercion. No such question of coercion arises with regard to legal rights, since rights are exercisable at will.

3. Other moral rights and duties where the issue of legal determination is one of moral indifference.

Conflict between law and morality arises either where the duties of law oppose the duties of morality, which face the moral believer with the alternatives of either breaking the law or acting against the principles of his moral code, or less sharply where a declared moral right of choice confronts an unqualified legal duty. While conflicts between the requirements of law and morality can arise only for those individuals who consciously accept the moral code concerned, other persons to whom the code addresses itself may be seen by believers as also having moral obligations to act in accordance with the code's requirements. Thus Catholics might assert that, while non-Catholics had no obligation to bring up their children as Catholics, or to refrain from voting Communist (for which Catholics might respectively be blamed and punished), they were held to be subject to blame or condemnation for having abortions. While the Catholic Church itself has no way of *enforcing* its moral view on abortion, Catholic doctors and nurses employed in the National Health Service might seek to give limited effect to the Church's moral position by refusing to carry out abortions. The contentious issue of the right of believers to seek to impose their own moral views on non-believers, without regard or reference to the law, is one of the most difficult raised by the right to strike.

So far rights and duties have been analysed in terms of law and morality, with a view to establishing those situations in which conflicts may arise and the nature of the conflict concerned. But few men in modern society live in a setting where all that confronts them is the problem of reconciling the requirements of the law and their personal moral code of conduct. Most men are associated with others in a variety of groups for different purposes and needs, where membership of such groups will establish distinctive group rights and duties. Such group rules of conduct are then liable to come into conflict with personal morality principles of some group members.

Since a group exists for specified purposes, and includes only a limited range of persons for limited periods of a particular activity, it is normally the case that the rights of members are limited to those things which are specifically permitted, or generally understood to be permitted. As a member of a trade union, for example, I have a right to do only those things which the rules and practices of the union permit. Consequently, the rights of group members (as distinct from the duties) are specified rights to do, or not to do, certain things. Such rights will either harmonize with, or at least not conflict with, the duty requirements of personal morality. However, one should recognize that, particularly in the field of trade unions, the quasi-legal rights of union members set down in the rules are in some crucial areas reinforced by unwritten, but well understood, internal quasi-moral injunctions to exercise the rights of the rulebook. Thus while the rules may say members have a *right* to attend branch meetings and take part in union elections, union morality preaches that members have a moral *duty* so to act. Since, however, the moral injunctions to exercise rights are not backed by sanctions, no difficulties normally arise for the member who on personal moral grounds feels compelled not to exercise his right. Problems are likely to arise only where union rules embody requirements imposed by law against the wishes of the unions and in opposition to popular union conceptions and values. Where this occurs there may be attempts by union activists to apply the principle of union morality rather than the union rule. So, for example, an individual who objects on principle to paying the political levy to the Labour Party may find some difficulty in a militant workshop in exercising his right under the terms of his union rules to 'contract out' of such payments – a right which unions are legally required to provide.

The most direct conflicts between personal morality and group membership will arise where the latter imposes a direct obligation, while personal morality either imposes a contrary duty or permits a choice. In the former case there is a fundamental contradiction between opposing duties. The conflict in the latter case is less clear-cut, likely to arise only if the person concerned exercises his right to act in a way contrary to that required of him by the group. If his determination of how to act in terms of personal morality coincides with the requirements of group obligation no conflict will appear, although a public affirmation of his *right* to decide whether or not to carry out group duties may itself generate opposition from other group members. Thus a union member who declared he had a right as an individual to decide whether or not to abide by an official strike call to all members, would be seen by most members as claiming something he had no right to – no right, that is, in terms of his position as a member of the union.

What is less obvious, and more important, is that the conflict between the requirements of group membership and the rights and duties of a member's personal morality may not be one which affects simply that member's conduct. In terms of his own moral code the member may see the situation as one of conflict between (a) himself and the group, (b) all believers and the group, or (c) all group members and the group. Thus one can envisage a situation (b) in which a Catholic trade unionist in one of the unions affiliated to the Confédération Française des Travailleurs Chrétiens might declare that all Catholics in the union had a duty to resist a union decision to strike in support of a general strike called by the Communist-led Confédération Générale du Travail, or (c) where a Communist in a non-Communist-led union might call on all union members to reject an executive decision to call off a national strike and return to work. It is important to note that in each of these cases we may have a situation where the individual Catholic or Communist is not simply expressing a personal viewpoint, but giving expression to determinations made by authoritative bodies in Church and Party held to be binding on all believers. In such cases the union may find itself in conflict, not simply with individual members but with other bodies to which these members adhere. Trade unions are liable to become the stamping grounds for different groups of members who associate together with a view to imposing their conceptions of policies on the union concerned. Thus for many years the Civil Service Clerical Association in Britain (later the Civil and Public Servants' Union) was bedevilled by struggles for power between Communist and Catholic activists. When this kind of situation exists there is not only the likelihood that the decisions of the union will be seen by the 'out-group' as the decisions of their opponents 'in office', but the possibility that in a crisis situation the ideological 'out-group' will deny the validity of the decisions of its 'opponents in office'. It may then call on all 'true' members of the union to carry out their 'real' duties to the union in the terms defined by the opposition, instead of the 'false' duties as defined by the enemies of the union at present in office.

Putting to one side the complication of sub-group crystallization and conflict, the underlying relationship of the group member to the group may be expressed in terms of reciprocal rights and duties. In a strike situation, for example, the union organization sees itself as having a *right* to call its members out, and those members a *duty* to respond; while the members will see themselves as having a *right* to receive, and the organization a *duty* to distribute, strike pay. The right to strike thus appears as a *right* of trade unions to strike and the *duty* of their members to respond to strike calls, except in those unions like the National Union of Mineworkers, where the members themselves have the right to decide whether or not to take national strike action. Even where the decision to strike is taken by strike ballot or, as happens with most local strikes, by a strike meeting, what we have is a collective decision by a body of persons to take collective action, where that collective decision is held to bind the participants. Thus the right to strike is unlike most other rights in that it is a collective right, not an individual right. An individual can neither decide to strike, nor take strike action except in association with others. In association, however, the individual can at most have a right to participate in the making of decisions about how the association should act, and he will be held to have a duty to the association to abide by the decisions reached. Thus, as far as a trade union is concerned, its individual members will have either a *duty* to strike or a *duty* not to strike in accordance with the decision made – never a *right* to strike. Many of the problems arising out of the right to strike arise out of its characteristic as a collective right. Anyone exercising his legal right not to strike undermines the effectiveness of the action of, and is consequently a threat to, those who exercise their right positively. Conflict is thus built into the right to strike in a way which does not operate with rights exercised by persons on a purely individual basis and in a personal context.

It is generally accepted that what distinguishes a right from a duty is that 'a right implies neither what a man must nor what he ought to do, but what he may do if he chooses';[3] and that in consequence a right to act necessarily involves a right not to act. However, while such a conclusion appears valid where the law is silent or morality indifferent, it is open to question where the law or morality specifically establishes a right. Where this occurs there is a change from the position where there was no right of A to X to one where A has a right to X. What is thereby established is a right to X, which A may or may not exercise as he thinks fit, rather than a right to X and a right not to X. Crucial to any determination of the precise nature of the right thus established will be the prior existing situation. Thus, prior to the passage of the Combination Acts of 1799 and 1800, no legal right of workmen to form combinations or trade unions had been established and in certain trades it was expressly forbidden. The absence of the legal right to combine meant that workers who did so were liable to prosecution on grounds of conspiracy in restraint of trade. With the passing of the Combination Acts all combinations of workmen for a wide range of trade union purposes were made

3. S. I. Benn, 'Rights', *The Encyclopedia of Philosophy*. The Macmillan Company and the Free Press, New York, 1967.

illegal; thereby imposing a duty on workmen not to enter trade unions and not to strike. Consequently, when the Combination Acts were repealed in 1825, along with the liability of criminal prosecution for conspiracy, what was clearly established in men's eyes was the legal right to combine and strike within the free area created by the removal of legal barriers. No question of workmen having a right not to combine together, or a right not to come out on strike, arose from these legal changes – indeed such conceptions were not meaningful, since in themselves *not* combining and *not* striking do not involve *doing* anything. But important issues of negative rights did arise in this sphere precisely because the right to combine and the right to strike are collective rights which can only be exercised by individuals acting together, in situations where *other* individuals may wish to exercise a right not to *join in* the combination or the strike. Thus the right not to combine and the right not to strike only emerge as individual claims for those faced with the prospect of an exercise by their fellow workers of the right to combine or to strike. Even, however, if the law had specifically laid down the right of individuals to decide for themselves whether to join a trade union and whether to go on strike, it is extremely doubtful whether such a negative legal right would have been recognized as *morally right* by most union members. In union thinking the right to join a trade union and the right to strike are accepted as rights against employers, whereas the rights not to join a union and not to strike are rights against one's fellow workers, and consequently unacceptable. The union interpretation is thus one where the legal rights to join unions and to strike become moral duties to go along with one's fellows.

MORAL CODES AND THE RIGHT TO STRIKE

In the first part of this chapter it was argued that the distinction between legal rights and moral rights, and between individual rights and group rights, was crucial to any understanding of the right to strike. But while legal rights and duties are the rights and duties of specific persons subject to the requirements of the laws of a particular state, moral rights and duties are expressed in terms of different moral conceptions and codes each claiming to be universally applicable. It is, therefore, necessary to examine the bearing of different moral approaches on the concept of a right to strike.

The first thing that has to be noted is the importance of the distinction between the morality of duty and the morality of aspiration, between the rules of conduct required of all men living in society and those rules of moral excellence which men should seek to follow in their quest for the Good Life. It is evident that it is only in terms of the former that a right to strike *in any form* could be established or accepted. Indeed the very idea of taking even protective action against another's aggression is contrary to the requirements of the higher morality. 'Return good for evil' or 'Do unto others as you would have them do unto you' are moral injunctions which individuals may seek to follow in their personal relationships, but they are incompatible with the existence of organizations like trade unions dedicated to the protection of their own rights and interests. A trade union cannot 'turn the other cheek' to an employer who cuts wage rates, without ceasing to be a trade union. Trade union members might find it possible to forgive the transgression of a lone member who failed to respond to a strike call, but they would find it hard, without jeopardizing their credibility and destroying the underlying principle of mutual solidarity, to forgive even a second transgression, let alone 'seventy times seven', transgressions. It is, therefore, necessary to confine our attention to those moral approaches enjoining behaviour which men may reasonably be expected to follow and reasonably be blamed for ignoring or thwarting; approaches which are relevant to, and not inherently incompatible with, the position of those engaged in protecting the common interests of workers.

The Right to Strike

Natural justice

Traditionally the moral conceptions held to govern economic relations between men in society were derived from the early Christian view of property as a trust held from God to be used for the common benefit. Aquinas writes, 'Whatever a man has in superabundance is owed, of natural right, to the poor for their sustenance', so that in dire necessity a man 'may take what is necessary from another person's goods either openly or by stealth'.[4] In these terms there could be no right of a man 'to do as he willed with his own', without regard to the needs of others, no right to take advantage of others' misfortune to drive the hardest bargain one could secure in the market place. The twin conceptions of 'just wages' and 'just prices' became firmly established in the public mind, finding official recognition in the regulation of wages and prices and, when that failed, popular expression in direct action to enforce justice. The poor felt themselves entitled as consumers to force merchants and shopkeepers to sell bread and other basic foods at 'fair' prices, and as workers to strike against employers to secure 'fair' wages. In May 1758 Thomas Percival, a Royston magistrate, charged the Manchester masters with responsibility for 'provoking the half-starved, half-clothed' check weavers to strike when they 'took advantage of the high prices of corn to sink wages'. The weavers themselves accepted that they 'should have no power ... to turn out' (i.e. to strike) if satisfactory machinery for the settlement of disputes could be established.[5]

We thus enter the industrial period with well-established conceptions of economic justice in terms of which trade unions and the strike weapon may be justified. The following principles might be adduced:

4. St Thomas Aquinas, *Summa Theologiae*, Secunda Secundae 21 Qu. 66, quoted in A. P. D'Entrèves, *Aquinas: Selected Political Writings*, Basil Blackwell, Oxford, 1954, p. 171.
5. Quoted in A. P. Wadsworth and Julia de L. Mann, *The Cotton Trade and Industrial Lancashire 1600–1780*, Manchester University Press, 1931, p. 362.

1. there is no inherent conflict of interest between employers and workers;
2. workers have a right to associate together to further the common interests of the members of a trade, having due regard to the general welfare of the community;
3. workers are entitled to receive, and employers a duty to pay, a 'fair day's wage for a fair day's work';
4. workers and employers should be encouraged to establish machinery for the peaceful resolution of their differences: alternatively the State itself might establish such machinery;
5. workers are entitled, as a last resort, to take strike action in support of a just grievance;
6. strikes (and lock-outs) must be conducted with due regard to the rights and interests of the community at large, and those of the opposing party.

It will be evident that on this approach the right to strike appears as a last-resort weapon, whose use can be most readily justified by good workers against bad employers in defence of established rights, or in furtherance of claims expressing minimum needs. These conditions were more commonly met in the nineteenth and early twentieth century than they are today.

While the approach outlined above finds authoritative expression in the moral teaching of the Catholic Church,[6] it is one which commands wide support both from trade unionists and non-unionists quite unconnected with that Church.

6. A lucid Catholic appraisal of strikes is provided by the Rev. Donald Alexander McLean, M.A.S.T.L., in *The Morality of the Strike*, P. J. Kennedy & Sons, New York, 1921. Father McLean quoted with approval Father Plater who declared, 'The working class of this country are suffering from suppressed Catholicism. The old pre-Reformation instincts for freedom and security have broken the husk of an un-Christian economic theory and practice – the selfish spirit of rationalistic capitalism' (p. 57). A more recent expression of Catholic views is to be found in the discussion statement, *The Right to Strike*, Catholic Truth Society, London, 1979, prepared by the Working Party on Human Rights established by the Catholic Bishops Conference of England and Wales.

The Right to Strike

Rawlsian justice

It is illuminating to compare the traditional precepts of natural justice with those embodied in John Rawl's *A Theory of Justice*, perhaps the most influential work on political theory to have appeared in recent years. Rawl's theory is one of positive justice secured by the consent of rational men concerned to secure not the common interest, but each his own self-interest. Such men might be induced to accept principles of justice by requiring them to agree upon the basic principles of the society in which they are to live, by requiring them to do so from behind a 'veil of ignorance' as to their present capacities or future social position and roles. Rawls believed that from such a position rational self-interested men would reach agreement on two basic principles – the principles of justice:

1. 'Each person is to have an equal right to the most extensive total system of equal basic liberties compatible with a similar system of liberty for all.'
2. 'Social and economic inequalities are to be arranged so that they are both (a) to the greatest benefit of the least advantaged, consistent with the just savings principle, and (b) attached to offices and positions open to all under conditions of fair equality of opportunity.'[7]

The first principle has priority over the second.

Critics of Rawls have argued that the two principles are too

7. John Rawls, *A Theory of Justice*, Harvard University Press, U.S.A., 1971, p. 302. He explains the just savings principle in the following terms:
'In attempting to estimate the fair rate of saving the persons in the original position ask what is reasonable for members of adjoining generations to expect of one another at each level of advance. They try to piece together a just savings schedule by balancing how much at each stage they would be willing to save for the immediate descendants against what they would feel entitled to claim of their immediate predecessors' (p. 289). The just savings principle 'is defined from the standpoint of the least advantaged in each generation ... In any generation their expectations are to be maximized subject to the condition of putting aside the savings that would be acknowledged [by them]' (p.272).

general to be of any use for resolving the specific issues facing men in modern industrial societies,[8] but this criticism may be at least partially met by combining the original position approach to the principles themselves. Thus a practice like striking may be held to be just if persons in the original position would have found it compatible with the two principles; that is to say if, given the relationship of capital and labour inherent in industrial society, they would as potential employers *or* workers have accepted that workers ought to have such a right. This approach might also be used to determine the legal conditions which should be attached to the right, as well as to decide when it would be morally right, in Rawlsian terms, to strike. Thus I would argue that the priority which Rawls attaches to the first principle over the second would rule out compulsory union membership or coercive picketing. On the other hand employers would be expected to accord to their workers terms and conditions not worse than those they would themselves be prepared to work for, and workers would be entitled to strike to secure such terms. The application of the second principle would deny legitimacy to strike action taken without regard to, and at the expense of, other less-advantaged groups of workers or of the public.

Rawlsian justice is more radical than natural justice since it requires not fair wages but a fair wages system, not the recognition of established economic rights and practices, but a reordering of society to secure the interests of the least advantaged. In this respect it has close affinities with Marxism, from which it differs, however, by the priority it accords to individual liberty.

---

8. See Robert Paul Wolff, *Understanding Rawls: A Reconstruction and Critique of a Theory of Justice*, Princeton University Press, U.S.A., 1977, Ch. 17; and John Schaar, 'Reflections on Rawls' Theory of Justice', *Social Theory and Practice*, Florida State University, U.S.A., Vol. 3, No. 1, Spring 1974.

The Right to Strike

Marxism

Although the question of whether Marxism should be treated as a moral doctrine is a matter of controversy, the rhetoric used by Marxists is one of moral exhortation. The Marxist approach may be expressed as follows. All members of the working class have an objective obligation, derived from a combination of historic destiny and social justice, to further the cause and interests of that class in its struggles against the bourgeoisie. All those, whatever their class position, who consciously identify themselves with the working-class cause, have a subjective obligation to do whatever they believe necessary to further that cause, where what is believed necessary is to be determined by reference to Marxist principles. Strikes are of especial concern for Marxists, since the strike weapon is by its nature a weapon of working-class struggle against the employing class. To assert the right to strike is thus for Marxists an assertion of the right of workers to fight capitalism. Consequently, while Marxists will accept that instances may arise where the workers are so weak that it may not be prudent to resort to strike action, or where the specific strike objective is contrary to working-class interests (e.g. to secure the dismissal of coloured workers), the underlying presumption is that strikes should be supported. It is through strikes that the working class most commonly and directly expresses its class interests, and through strike experience that it gains class consciousness. In most industrial conflicts, therefore, there will be an obligation on Marxists to take the initiative in urging strike action; while in all but those with class-distorted objectives, there will be an obligation to support strike action already taken.

It is important to stress that this Marxist approach to strikes as a means of working-class struggle is characteristic of many trade unionists who are not avowed Marxists. Indeed one might go further and say that the conception of strikes as a legitimate weapon to be used by the workers in their struggles with the employers is the predominant view of organized industrial workers. Most workers can consequently be appealed to in terms of working-class solidarity against their employers in a strike situation, even though such appeals may sometimes be overridden by other considerations or other loyalties.

Two further points are worth a brief mention. Firstly, in contrast to Catholicism, with Marxism we have no single recognized source of authority. Consequently, different Marxist groups may not only urge the workers to take different courses of action in a major industrial dispute, but may attack their rivals for 'playing into the hands of the ruling class'. Secondly, since Marxist groups seek to direct the actions of their own members in industrial disputes, attempts to impose a particular line of action in a strike situation may evoke opposition from other workers who resent what they see as 'outside' interference. Marxist groups, however, are very ready to assert their right to provide the workers with the leadership 'objectively' required. In so far as such leadership is designed to further realization of the strategic objective of overthrowing capitalism it may come into conflict with the more limited objectives of the ordinary striker.

The following Marxist precepts may be adduced:

1. Workers have a right to take strike action whenever they think it will be to their advantage to do so.
2. Workers have a duty to come out on strike whenever vital working-class interests are at stake.
3. Workers ought not to strike in furtherance of objectives which are incompatible with, or which retard, the class struggle against capitalism.
4. Class-conscious workers have a duty to try to gain the leadership of any strike and to so conduct it that the general level of class consciousness of the strikers is raised.

Economic individualism

In contrast to Marxism which asserts that the interests of all can only be secured if workers further their own *real* economic class interests, the classical economists taught that such a common interest would be secured if every man pursued his own *actual*

29

economic interests. Economic individualism is a doctrine of the natural identity of economic interest between the individual and society, secured through the operation of the laws of supply and demand operating freely in the market place. The doctrine had the twin merits of simplicity and attractiveness: a man ought to pursue, what he was in any case inclined to pursue, his own selfish interests.

It is readily apparent that such teaching had a particular appeal to the thrusting entrepreneur. It provided him with moral justification for running his own business in his own way and for opposing union activities as interference both with his rights and with the free play of market forces, to the detriment of the community at large. But it would be a mistake to see economic individualism as a doctrine which only the employers adopted. Large numbers of workers were, and are, opposed to trade unions because they believe either that union interference with a free labour market is to everyone's disadvantage, or that they personally would do better than their weaker brothers in a free market. Economic individualists in the early nineteenth century were divided over whether unions and strikes should be legally prohibited, but were united in holding them to be not only economically harmful but morally wrong. They saw unions as bodies aiming at the frustration of the basic rights of individuals as employers or workers to decide for themselves the terms and conditions on which they would make their labour or capital available, and the strike as a weapon of coercion. State action was, therefore, required to protect the rights of individuals and to maintain the free market.

Individual rights and the minimal State

The Achilles' heel of economic individualism was its grounding of individual rights on the principle of the natural identity of economic interest between the individual and the community – the confident assertion that an economic 'free-for-all' was good for everyone. As the gap between principle and reality became ever more apparent, support for the principle declined. The 'night-watchman' state, restricted to the protection of rights and the free market, did not secure the common good and came to be replaced by the welfare State in which the rights of the individual were required to give way to the greatest happiness of the greatest number.

This approach has itself recently come under strong attack, in particular by Robert Nozick in *Anarchy, State and Utopia*. Nozick asserts the primacy of individual rights and argues that the only State which can be justified in terms of such rights is a minimal State 'limited to the narrow functions of protection against force, theft, fraud, enforcement of contracts and so on'; a State which 'may not use its coercive apparatus for the purpose of getting some citizens to aid others, or in order to prohibit activities to the people for their *own* good or protection'.[9]

It is not possible to apply Nozick's analysis as it stands to the right to strike since he makes no reference to, or provision for, groups like trade unions within his minimal State. This deficiency may be remedied, however, by laying down two extension principles:

1. Individuals are entitled to, but must not be required to, associate together for any purposes permitted to individuals.

9. Robert Nozick, *Anarchy, State and Utopia*, Basil Blackwell, Oxford, 1974, p. ix. In Chapter 7 Nozick sets out his historical entitlement theory of holdings (i.e. the resources which different persons control) — 'the holdings of a person are just if he is entitled to them by the principles of justice in acquisition and transfer, or of the principle of rectification of injustice (as specified by the first two principles)' (p. 153). Unfortunately Nozick does not attempt to formulate the principle of justice in acquisition and confines himself to indicating some of the difficult problems raised by the principle of rectification of injustice. What Nozick provides are the general outlines of a theory of justice in holdings. A theory specifying each of the three principles of justice in holdings would be required before one could seek to establish whether any particular set or pattern of holdings (with its associated legal rights) was justified. Until this is done, not only is it impossible to determine what the individual rights are which the minimal State should protect, but, more crucially, whether a more-than-minimal State is required if the rectification of injustice in holdings and rights is to be secured.

2. The State may only intervene with groups to protect either the groups' own members or outsiders (whether individuals or other groups) from the perpetration of force, theft, fraud, or to secure the enforcement of contracts.

The extension principles are compatible with voluntary, but not compulsory, trade unionism, requiring members under specific conditions to abide by decisions collectively arrived at. In relation to strikes, such decisions would have to be made in accordance with the terms of contracts of employment and any agreed collective bargaining procedures, and would be morally binding on union members only. Individuals who were not union members would be morally entitled to remain at work during a strike or to take the place of strikers. Unions would be permitted to negotiate on behalf of union members only – other workers would be entitled to work on such terms as they thought fit. The State would be required to keep out of collective bargaining (other than for its own employees), except when intervention was necessary to maintain the rights of individual workers.

In these terms the rights of the individual may be asserted against those of the paternalist welfare State, without reliance on the benevolent 'hidden hand' of free market forces, as with economic individualism.

Moral realism

The various approaches considered so far have all embodied principles or conceptions of rightness or justice which it is claimed men ought to seek to give effect to, to answer the questions 'Ought workers to have a right to strike?' and 'When are workers entitled to take strike action?' There remains, however, a very different and influential approach which I have termed 'moral realism' which would hold such questions to be wrongly posed. Moral realism may take one of two forms: either a denial of the possibility of making valid moral judgements, or a denial that moral judgements and moral considerations have any relevance outside our personal lives and in our purely personal relations. The upshot, however, is the same in either case. What moral realism presents is an analysis of industrial conflict in terms of power. Free collective bargaining is a process whereby unions and employers each seek to ascertain the other's bargaining strength and concession limit, with a view to determining its own negotiating tactics. A strike is the result of a miscalculation of the power position by those negotiating, with either the union or the employer underestimating the other's strength. The role of the conciliator or mediator in an industrial dispute is exactly the same as that of the negotiators themselves – to ascertain and make plain to all concerned what the actual power situation requires as a settlement. Claims of justice are irrelevant to the outcome of an industrial dispute, though the existence of a strong sense of commitment to a claim as just has to be taken into account in the power calculation, since those who believe their cause to be just fight harder than those who do not. Workers are 'entitled' to strike when they have good reason to believe they can win.

Moral realism requires us to recognize that the law relating to strikes, and the mode of its application by the authorities, must itself be expected to reflect the relative strength of the parties concerned. One should not be surprised to find both that the union position in strikes is much stronger than it was forty or fifty years ago, and that increased union power has given rise to demands from those adversely affected for such power to be curbed. Moral realists, however, would counsel caution on those who would seek to redress the legal industrial balance of power by legal intervention on the side of weaker parties, whether they be employers or the public.

In the following chapters I shall attempt to show the bearing of these approaches on some of the major problems raised by, or inherent in, the right to strike, looking first at the historical setting in which unions and strikes emerge as issues of public concern.

Two

Workers and Unions

The emergence of combinations or unions of journeymen and workmen was a feature of the changing pattern of economic life in the eighteenth century. As the century wore on the guild system decayed, creating a class of journeymen with little or no hope of ever becoming 'masters'. These skilled workers resorted to combination to protect and further their interests against the now separate class of employers, either by the direct enforcement of their demands by 'go-slows' and 'turn-outs' (strikes) or by petitioning Parliament for the redress of grievances and the regulation of wages. Although combinations were widely held to be conspiracies in restraint of trade at common law, specifically forbidden by statute in particular trades, they grew rapidly. In the same period *laissez faire* doctrines increasingly came to dominate the thinking of members of the House of Commons. The issue came to a head during the French Wars when Parliament rescinded the long-standing legislative provisions for protecting trades from unfair competition and for regulating conditions within trades; while at the same time enacting legislation forbidding all combinations, whether of workmen or employers. Combinations were seen by Parliament, and the propertied classes it represented, as both economically harmful and politically dangerous in a period of social unrest and radical fervour. The prevailing official view was forcefully expressed by Lord Justice Armadale in 1808 at the trial of striking Scottish journeymen papermakers. 'In such a country as this,' he declared, 'depending upon due subordination of all ranks and orders, in a country extended and extending, by means of that mutual and necessary relation betwixt masters and workmen, I cannot figure any crime more ruinous, dangerous and tremendous in its consequences to pass unpunished.'[1]

In spite, however, of formal legal proscription in the Combination Laws of 1799 and 1800, combinations continued to flourish; and strikes, sometimes accompanied by violence and intimidation against both masters and workmen, were a common feature of the industrial scene. The Government of the day, however, lacked the resources necessary to instigate prosecutions on a large scale, and most employers were unwilling or unready to do so. By 1824 Parliament was prepared to listen to those who urged a different policy. Francis Place, the author and orchestrator of repeal, found a sympathetic response to his claim that strikes and the associated violence were in large measure a direct consequence of forcing workers' combinations underground. Place, indeed, went further, declaring that with repeal, 'Combinations will soon cease to exist. Men have been kept together for long periods only by the oppression of the laws.'[2] The influential Liberal journal, the *Edinburgh Review*, championed repeal on the economic ground that without restrictions market forces would ensure that wages never rose above 'their natural and proper rate'.[3] The Parliamentary Select Committee endorsed these sentiments, recommending repeal as a step towards 'that perfect freedom which ought to be allowed to each party of employing his labour or capital in the manner he may deem most advantageous'.[4]

1. *Reports from the Select Committee on Artisans and Machinery*, H.M.S.O., 1824, pp. 492–3. Appendix A, 'Extract from Mr Hutchinson's Book' on the trial of James Taylor and other journeymen papermakers, Edinburgh, 1808.

2. Francis Place to Sir Francis Burdett, 25 June 1825, quoted in Sidney and Beatrice Webb, *The History of Trade Unionism 1666–1920*, printed by the authors for the Trade Unionists of the United Kingdom, Christmas 1919, p. 109.

3. 'Combination Laws and Restraints on Immigration', the *Edinburgh Review*, January 1824, Vol. XXIX.

4. *Resolutions of the Select Committee on Artisans and Machinery*, H.M.S.O., 1824.

What the Committee failed to face up to was 'that perfect freedom' would inevitably lead to deep industrial conflict, given the prevailing economic conditions and sharply opposing views of workers and employers as to the ways in which, and purposes for which, that freedom should be used. The great upsurge of combination and strike activity which followed on repeal in 1824 brought this inherent conflict to the fore, producing strident employer demands for the re-imposition of legal sanctions. The dominant *laissez-faire* view of the political establishment and of 'enlightened' employers was admirably expressed by William Huskisson, who embodied both positions in his own person. Speaking in the House of Commons as President of the Board of Trade he declared that workers 'were at liberty to take all proper means to secure that remuneration for their labour to which they conceived they were entitled – considering the circumstances of a great demand for labour, or a great expense incurred in the purchase of provisions. Under circumstances of this nature they might reasonably ask for higher wages.' If the workers stopped there the workings of the laws of supply and demand would determine whether their demands would be met by the employer. Unfortunately, however, workers 'did not stop there', said Huskisson. 'They combined for purposes of the most objectionable description: they should conduct their business: they combined to dictate whether the master should take an apprentice or not: they combined for the purpose of preventing certain individuals from working: they combined to dictate to their masters the mode in which they combined to enforce the principle that wages should be paid alike to every man, whether he were a good workman or a bad one, and they levied heavy fines on those who refused to agree to their conditions.'[5]

There was nothing new in these 'objectionable' purposes. The London journeymen hatters in the 1770s had successfully kept down the number of apprentices their masters could take and

5. *Parliamentary Debates New Series*, Hansard, 3 May 1825, Vol. XIII, cols. 354–5.

compelled them to dismiss men who would not join the union.[6] Even in front of the 1825 House of Commons Select Committee, charged with the task of reviewing the repeal of the Combination Laws, worker representatives defended the traditional union stance. In reply to the question 'Do you conceive that you had a right to prevent the masters from taking apprentices for whatever number of years they chose?', George Rippon, a South Shields shipwright, replied, 'I do not conceive we have a right to dictate to them in that manner, but however we thought it was an injury to us, and we thought it our right to do the best for ourselves we could.' While denying that the shipwrights had a rule which forbad working with non-union labour – 'every man is left to himself' – Rippon stated quite categorically, that he would not work with non-union men and expressed his conviction that the rest of the workers in the yard would refuse to do so.[7]

In the event the amendments to the law introduced in 1825 followed closely along the lines indicated by Huskisson in his speech to the Commons. The purpose of combinations was narrowed to questions of wages and hours of labour and more stringent restrictions were imposed to prevent violence and intimidation, including prohibitions on 'molestation' and 'obstruction' which if rigidly enforced would have precluded peaceful picketing. Consequently, trade unions found themselves faced with the alternatives of either restricting themselves to action within the law, at the expense of what they saw as their member's necessary and legitimate interests, or ignoring the legal restrictions while taking advantage of their limited legal status. Not surprisingly most of them opted for the latter course – seeking to give effect to the right to combine and strike which they were convinced they ought to have, rather than the legal right guaranteed to them. In 1869 the Commission on Trade Unions in Britain reported:

6. A. P. Wadsworth and Julia de L. Mann, *The Cotton Trade and Industrial Lancashire 1600–1780*, Manchester University Press, 1931, p. 381.

7. *Report from the Select Committee on the Combination Laws*, H.M.S.O., 1825, Vol. IV, pp. 341–2.

No trades union, so far as our observation has extended, has attempted to give to the combination a wholly legal character by confining the application of its funds in support of men on strike to the limits within which combinations were legalized ... Unions contemplated generally the application of the funds to the support of men engaged in a strike for the purpose of enforcing some decision come to by the union as to what they deem to be the interests of trade. Many such strikes would therefore be unlawful combinations at common law, and would not be relieved by the statute.[8]

While the repeal of the Combination Acts meant that employers lost their legal right to instigate criminal proceedings against workers who combined or took strike action, they retained the right to instigate proceedings and secure imprisonment of workmen for conspiracy in restraint of trade or breach of contract: employees in breach of contract were liable to imprisonment by the criminal courts, employers to pay damages awarded by the civil courts. This privileged employer position was defended on the grounds that, since most employees had no resources, employers would be put at a severe disadvantage if they had to rely on damages from the civil courts. The argument prevailed until 1867. Seven years more were to pass before the right of employers to promote the prosecution of strikers for criminal conspiracy was removed, in the face of rigorous opposition from the National Federation of Associated Employers of Labour which embraced many of the leading industrialists of the period. The Association expressed outright hostility to the principle of unionization:

What we want is that workmen should be isolated as employers or tradesmen or professional men are, and no more. The middle classes are free; we wish to see the working classes, equally free ... A man has only his labour to sell. Let him take it on the open market and get the most he can for it. If he can get more

8. *Eleventh and Final Report of the Commissioners Appointed to Inquire into the Organisation and Rules of Trade Unions and Other Associations,* H.M.S.O., 1869, Vol. 1, pp. xix-xx.

than others, or sees an opening in which it would be to his advantage to take less, he must be at liberty to make his bargain as he chooses . . .[9]

It is ironic that the principle of legal equality before the criminal law was opposed by powerful employers acting in association and claiming to champion the rights of the individual worker. But although the cause they espoused might be suspect, the sentiments they expressed had wide appeal and support. The repeal of the Combination Laws did not reflect approval for the principle of combination over that of individual action. It was rather that the principle of freedom of individual action seemed incompatible with a total proscription on individual masters or workmen associating together to further their common individual purposes. Economic combinations might not be beneficial in themselves, but as long as they did not act in restraint of trade, or in breach of contract, they might be tolerated.

The legal position after 1825 was that employees were at liberty to join trade unions and employers were at liberty to refuse employment to union members. Where the latter occurred union members might either seek employment elsewhere, or attempt through strike action to persuade their employer to change his mind on the issue of union membership. Legislators, lawyers and judges saw no inherent contradiction here, since the law had not established, and never contemplated, a right of combination overriding the rights of economic proprietorship. My right to join a union was a purely personal *liberty* right against the State, not a *claim* right against my employer. Even staunch union members did not assert that employers ought to be deprived of their legal right to refuse to employ union workmen. Such a legal change was inconceivable in the nineteenth century. Morally the union position could be better expressed in the weaker form 'employers ought not to exercise their legal rights to refuse to employ union

9. *Capital and Labour*, 18 March 1874, quoted in W. Hamish Fraser, *Trade Unions and Society: The Struggle for Acceptance 1850–1880*, Allen & Unwin, 1974, p. 118.

workmen', than in the stronger form 'employers have a moral duty not to exercise their legal right to employ union workmen'; since it was difficult for them to find a moral foundation for such a strict duty, except in conceptions, like Owenism, which denied the validity of industrial society as it then existed. It was possible, however, to assert that for an employer to exercise his unquestioned legal right of dismissal of unionists was 'unfair', as it meant that workers were heavily penalized for exercising *their* legal right to join unions. A man ought to lose his job only if he did something wrong, or if trade conditions made dismissals inevitable.

Employers were for the most part disinclined to see matters in this light. Throughout the nineteenth century, and indeed beyond, there were constant attacks by employers on the principles and practice of trade unionism. The following charges were commonly levelled:

1. Trade unions were economically harmful.
(a) They existed to impose restrictions on the free market in labour.
(b) They opposed the introduction of labour-saving machinery.
(c) They applied restrictive practices which adversely affected production.

2. Trade unions were socially harmful.
(a) They encouraged workmen to think in class terms and to see their interests as opposed to those of their employers.
(b) The class conflict and hatred which unions preached encouraged political extremism.
(c) Trade unions encouraged strikes which were the cause of much public inconvenience, disturbance of the peace, and violence against non-strikers.

3. Trade unions interfered with the rights of employers.
(a) They were based on a denial of the basic right of employers to run their businesses in their own way.
(b) Their aim was to force the employer, by threat of strike action, to accept *their* terms for the employment of labour.

4. Trade unions interfered with the rights of workers.
(a) They sought to coerce workers into joining trade unions and coming out on strike.
(b) They denied the right of the individual worker to make his own personal contract of employment with the employer, and wanted the poor worker to be paid the same as the good worker.

There is a strong element of reality in almost all these assertions, but that reality only appears as objective truth when viewed from the traditional employer standpoint. If, as virtually all early Victorian employers believed, masters had an unqualified right to run their businesses in their own way (subject only to the minimal requirements of the law), and if free competition was the recipe for prosperity, then trade unions *were* undesirable organizations. Even those masters who themselves employed union labour, from considerations of advantage or conviction rather than *force majeure*, did not deny that unions, especially in some trades and areas, exhibited highly undesirable features. The acceptance or approval of unions by such employers was normally accorded 'on balance', rather than 'on principle'. They were thus disinclined to deny that their fellow employers were justified in taking a different view of where their advantage or duty lay. Such restraint was in large measure absent amongst those who refused to employ union labour. Since unions in their view exhibited the evil characteristics outlined above, they constituted a threat to society in general, and the employing class in particular. Employers as a class were therefore seen as having a moral duty not to exercise their legal liberty right to employ union labour, since this would open the road to union domination, and with it the loss of the master's right of self-determination within the workshop.

The mode of argument put forward by the employers was the antithesis of that of the trade unions. The former asserted an identity of interest between masters and workers, and a conflict of interests between workers and trade unions: the latter a conflict of interests between masters and workers, and an identity of interests between workers and trade unions. In the first instance, workers were seen as individuals, each of whom had an interest in getting the best price he could for his labour on the open market: in the second, they appear as members of a class or trade whose interests could be furthered only by collective action. Each held the others' view to be fallacious. But, while masters thought that union workmen had been led, or come to accept, a mistaken view of their true interests as workmen, unions saw the masters' view as essentially a mask consciously designed to mislead the workers. There seems, however, little reason to doubt that the anti-union masters did believe that non-unionism was in the workers' interests, *as they saw and understood them*. The real interests of masters and men could only be protected if employers resisted the spread of trade unionism by employing only non-union labour. The legal liberty rights of the employer not to employ union labour, and of the worker not to join a trade union, had to be asserted *against* the legal liberty rights to employ union labour and to join trade unions. While these two sets of liberty rights might have equal legal validity, they did not appear as having equal moral validity in the eyes of most employers.

It is readily apparent that from the union standpoint the dominant employer view constituted a direct threat and challenge to their existence. The non-union shop required unionists either to conceal or renounce their membership or to seek employment elsewhere; but if non-union shops became general, as militant employers hoped, the legal right to belong to trade unions would cease to be exercisable. The necessary minimum condition for that liberty right to be meaningful was that in every industry there should be a substantial number of employers prepared to employ union labour. To establish that condition it was vital to resist attempts to impose or extend the application of the principle of non-unionism. Union power had to be exerted, and the moral rights of workers asserted, against employers who sought to prevent their employees joining trade unions. The latter task was far from easy, since many of the anti-union sentiments held by employers were shared by the middle and upper classes, whose views constituted the public opinion of the time. To take one example, during the 1859–60 London builders' strike the masters sought to impose the 'document' (as the renunciation of union membership was known) on strikers as a condition of re-engagement. This document read, 'I declare that I am not now, nor will I during the continuance of my engagement with you become, a member of, or support any society which directly or indirectly interferes with the arrangements of this or any other establishment, or the hours or terms of labour; and that I recognize the right of employers and employed individually to make any trade engagements on which they may choose to agree.'[10]

This position was approved of by *The Times*, and by Lord St Leonards, ex-Conservative Lord Chancellor, since it left the workman 'at perfect liberty to strike for wages' ... 'but that he must act upon his own free will, and not submit to the orders and regulations of any society'. 'A central committee of a trade', continued Lord St Leonards, 'with all its branches issuing its mandate for a strike, which all members must obey under severe penalties, and which, in truth, compelled them to coerce, as far as they can, working men who are not members, with whom they will not work unless they pay fines and become members, is an odious, an insufferable tyranny, which degrades the free men of England into mere slaves.' But as Lord St Leonards recognized, it was a tyranny which 'vast masses voluntarily placed themselves under ...'[11] It did not occur to St Leonards that vast masses might think it a tyranny that an employer should be able to face them with the forced choice between giving up their legal rights to belong to a trade union, and being prevented from working in the building

10. Quoted in R. and E. Frow and M. Katanka, *Strikes: A Documentary History*, Charles Knight, 1971, p. 85.

11. *The Times*, 13 December 1859. Lord St Leonards nevertheless urged the London master builders to withdraw the 'document' to which the building workers were resolutely opposed, and instead to have a statement of the law relating to trade unions put up in every workshop.

trades in London. Where workers signed the 'document' in order to secure their jobs, as engineers did after the successful lock-out of 1852, many refused to abandon their union and simply kept their membership secret. It is an illuminating reflection on the climate of opinion of the time that, while the union publicly declared that promises made under duress were invalid, even such a friend of labour as Thomas Hughes, the Christian Socialist, was deeply upset at what he saw as an 'inexcusable' act of bad faith.[12] Fortunately for the trade unions, there were influential persons outside the unions who saw the moral issue as one stemming from the doubtful nature of the 'document' itself. Charles Dickens, in his report on the Preston spinners' strike 1853–4, characterized the attempt by 'the respectable combined body of Preston masters' to lay down 'the principle that no man should be employed henceforth who belonged to any combination', as 'partial and unfair'.[13] Twenty years earlier Richard Oastler, the Tory radical, had denied that employers were morally entitled to require workmen to abandon a right 'which the law and Nature gave them, the RIGHT of uniting for mutual protection'.[14]

'The document' was only one of a number of morally doubtful, but legally valid, weapons which nineteenth-century employers deployed against their workmen in major industrial disputes. In the mining villages and small towns, which were economically and socially dominated by the coal-owners, strikers' families were evicted from their 'tied' houses, shopkeepers pressurized not to grant credit, and Poor Law Unions induced to refuse relief. Such actions were practised and defended by employers who were opposed to the principle of trade unionism. In their eyes employers were fully justified in using any means not proscribed by law to defeat the economically dangerous and socially divisive tendencies represented by workers' combinations. Indeed it might be

12. Sidney and Beatrice Webb, op. cit., p. 216.

13. Charles Dickens, 'On Strike', *Household Words*, 11 February 1854, *Miscellaneous Papers*, Vol. I.

14. Richard Oastler, 'A Serious Address to the Mill Owners, Manufacturers and Cloth-Dressers of Leeds', Huddersfield, 1834.

argued that, in the absence of State proscription of trade unions, it was the social duty of employers to resist the threat to property and authority which unions represented and embodied. It was unreasonable and foolish for outsiders, ignorant of the facts of industrial life, to challenge the moral right of employers to exercise to the full their legal right to combat unions and local strikes.

Not all employers, however, took this view. A. J. Mundella, the Nottingham hosiery manufacturer, was one of an increasing number of employers who supported the growth of 'responsible' trade unionism, with a legitimate and useful role to perform in society. It was the 'responsible' attitude of the new stable unions of engineers and carpenters, and the positive response of 'enlightened' employers, which led *The Times* (formerly a bitter critic of trade unionism) at the end of the sixties to declare that unions should be given 'free scope for legitimate development'.[15] This view grew rapidly stronger, and in 1875 not one voice was raised in the Commons to oppose two major Conservative Bills – one to abolish workers' liability to imprisonment for breach of contract and the other to legalize peaceful picketing.

The eclipse of the 'document', the legalization of peaceful picketing, and the removal of liability for criminal conspiracy proceedings for taking strike action, while strengthening the position of the unions, left employers' rights legally virtually unchanged, and morally virtually unchallenged, by respectable and respected opinion. A strike was legally and popularly seen as a collective determination of individual contracts of employment, and a 'struck' employer was therefore fully entitled to find other sources of labour to keep his plant in operation. The measures he might take included:

1. Dismissing strikers and requiring returning workers to apply for re-engagement.
2. Recruiting replacement labour either (a) temporarily to break the strike, or (b) permanently as replacements for the strikers.

15. *The Times*, 8 July 1869.

3. Circulating black lists of strikers to prevent their obtaining other employment.
4. Protecting non-strikers from harassment by strikers.
5. Requiring men belonging to a non-striking trade to undertake work normally done by men of a striking trade.

The exercise of any of these rights by an employer inevitably aroused strong union and striker opposition – opposition which had its root in a fundamental difference of view about the nature of the employment relationship as seen in law and in trade union thinking. The latter was based on a refusal to accept that employers had a moral right to hire and fire at will, as distinct from at necessity. Workers were thought to have a right to their jobs, subject only to good behaviour and the vicissitudes of trade. A strike was, on this view, not to be seen as a collective determination of contracts of employment, but as a temporary stoppage of work by workers seeking an improvement in the conditions of, or remuneration for, *their* jobs. Sacking strikers, with the express or implicit requirement that the returning strikers would have to apply individually for re-engagement, constituted a severe challenge to the worker's concept of being a person with rights in and to his job.

It was precisely because for workers a strike was *not* a collective determination of contracts of employment, that strikers could not, and did not, accept the right of employers to engage alternative labour, since this meant giving *their* jobs to others. Workers were unwilling to accept, even if they were unable to refute, the implications of the principles of political economy as then established. The only valid purpose of a strike, political economy taught, was to test the state of the market for labour. 'But,' declared the *Edinburgh Review*,

instead of suffering that issue to be fairly tried, the Unionists in fact armed themselves with another weapon, which destroys all equality between the contending forces. The real question being whether the masters can get other labour in the market on the terms which their own workmen refuse to take, the men in defiance of law and justice prevent by the strong arm other labour from offering itself. They exclude the action of demand and supply by forcibly cutting off supply . . . This they do by the abominable practice of 'Picqueting' . . .[16]

It is not difficult to understand the unwillingness of striking workmen to accept the claimed moral force of the laws of supply and demand, reinforcing as they did the economic interests of the employers. The reality of 'an appeal to the market' was first the attempt to find local replacement labour, and, where this failed, the importation of outside strike-breakers, escorted *en masse* under heavy police protection to the struck works, where they were fed and housed until the strike ended. Such factory-incarcerated labour, often of Irish or foreign origin, was both physically and spiritually immune to precisely that form of peaceful picketing which the Conspiracy and Protection of Property Act 1875 had legalized. If any substantial number of employers succeeded in establishing access to a permanent pool of professional strike-breakers, then, not only would the legal right to picket be effectively nullified, but the way would be open to undermining trade union organization. This was indeed the thinking which lay behind the various attempts, particularly in the shipping industry and docks industry, to set up 'free' labour associations, and which culminated in the establishment of the National Free Labour Association in 1893 and the Free Labour Protection Association in 1897.[17] By defeating a major strike the employers might hope to break the power of the unions for some years, especially if the

16. The *Edinburgh Review*, October 1867, Vol. CXXVI, p. 447.

17. *The Report of the Proceedings of the Free Labour Protection Association*, July 1897, records 'the officials of the Association have satisfied themselves in every case where non-union workmen have been engaged for firms in various parts of the country, that police protection could be obtained if necessary. In such cases where such protection was not immediately forthcoming, the Association has been prepared to draft an adequate force of trained and experienced men into the district to picket the pickets, and to ensure protection to non-unionists. The Association has at its command a large number of trained men, ex-guardsmen etc.; and 800 men who have served full-time in the City and Metropolitan Police Forces.'

defeat was sufficiently decisive to permit the weeding-out of trade union militants from amongst those offered re-employment.

Faced with the mass importation of outside labour, strikers were forced to choose between defeat and a resort to violence to force the 'blacklegs' to withdraw; where defeat might mean the loss of the strikers' jobs and livelihood. Many of the most serious cases of striker-violence in the nineteenth century stemmed from the large-scale use of imported strike-breaking labour. During the 1867 miners' strike in South Lancashire, for example, 5,000 colliers marched to Wigan smashing pit property at every pit still at work, and driving out blacklegs imported from Staffordshire.[18] Striking workers were concerned to deny to employers their legal right to replace them. The moral right to strike as understood by workers in the nineteenth century, in opposition to nineteenth-century employers, judges and newspaper proprietors, always included the basic moral right not to have one's place taken by another, irrespective of what the law might say. It is interesting to note that the *Eleventh Report of the Commission on the Organisation and Rules of Trade Unions and Other Associations* (1869), whilst strongly condemning picketing, accepted that, 'It is hardly in human nature that the pickets who are interested parties, and who are suffering the privations incident to the strike, should always keep within the limits of representation and persuasion, when dealing with men whom they see about to undertake the work which they have refused, and who may thus render the strike abortive.'[19]

But it was not only outsiders who were seen as legitimate targets for attack by pickets; there was an equal readiness in many trades, especially mining, to use coercion or threats of coercion against any workers who exercised their legal right not to heed a strike call. The old Durham ballad 'The Blackleg Miner'

18. Raymond Challinor, *The Lancashire and Cheshire Miners*, Frank Gresham, Newcastle upon Tyne, 1972, pp. 78–9.

19. *Eleventh and Final Report of the Commissioners Appointed to Inquire into the Organisation and Rules of Trade Unions and Other Associations*, H.M.S.O., 1869, Vol. I, p. xxi.

expresses a sentiment widely and deeply held by trade unionists right down to the present:

> O don't go near the Sedgehill mine
> For across the mainway they hang a line
> To catch the throat and break the spine
> Of the dirty blackleg miners.
>
> They take your tools and your duds as well
> And throw them down in the pit of hell
> It's down you go and fare you well
> You dirty blackleg miners.
>
> So join the union while you may
> Don't you wait till your dying day
> For that may not be far away
> You dirty blackleg miners.[20]

THE DUTY TO BELONG TO A UNION

Trade unionism is incompatible with economic individualism whether practised by employer or worker. The right to belong to a trade union, unlike the right to belong to a religious sect, is one which inherently involves interference with the rights of others. An employer who is prepared to employ union workmen has to be prepared to face demands for the implementation of union rates and conditions. In the nineteenth century this commonly took the form of presenting wage lists drawn up by the unions, since jointly negotiated rates were rare. Union men were expected to work for not less than union rates, and since it was not practical to pay union rates to union members and to settle individual rates with non-unionists, the acceptance of the right of individual workmen to join trade unions came to mean the loss of the right of employers to pay, and of employees to accept, such wages as they thought fit. But, while non-unionists might view with regret this

20. R. and E. Frow and M. Katanka, op. cit., p. 55.

loss of their right individually to determine their conditions of employment, unionists increasingly came to resent what they saw as the indefensible moral position of the non-unionist. Trade unions could not be satisfied with the withdrawal by employers of restrictions on their workers belonging to trade unions, leaving each worker with the moral right to decide for himself whether to become a member. Far from having a negative moral right to cut themselves off from their union colleagues, non-members were seen as having a positive moral duty to enrol. In terms of the underlying principle of working-class solidarity the assertion of a moral duty of membership is not the duty of workers who as individuals benefit from the actions of other individuals, but of workers who as members of a group benefit from the actions of their own colleagues. Non-unionists are not so much men who fail to see where their personal interests lie, as men who refuse to recognize or understand that their true interests lie in furthering the welfare of the collectivity of which they are a part. The assertion of a moral duty of union membership rests on three propositions:

1. Trade unions further the interests of all workers.
2. Non-unionists benefit from the action of trade unions.
3. Non-unionism weakens trade unions in their struggles to further workers' interests.

But these propositions are not self-evident truths even for those who reject a self-interested individualistic position. Thus it might be charged that, since it is possible for a union to fail to further the interests of its members, each individual worker has the right to decide whether or not any particular union meets this requirement, entitling it to his membership. Even more controversially it might be claimed that unions serve immoral purposes since, in furthering the sectional interests of their own group of workers, they ignore or even undermine the general interests, or the interests of the weakest members of the community.

Even, however, if the three propositions are accepted, it does not follow that a moral duty of union membership is established, since that conclusion rests on the questionable assumption that obligations are created by conferred benefits even when· involuntarily or accidentally conferred. It is surely of the very nature of voluntary activity that it benefits persons other than those who participate in its work. Thus it might be argued that all the unemployed in Britain during the 1930s benefited from the strenuous efforts of the Unemployed Workers Movement, but it is only in a weak or conditional sense that one might have asserted that all unemployed workers *ought* to have joined the Movement. Unemployed workers generally might perhaps have been said to have a prudential obligation to join, in so far as further benefits might be held to depend on the Movement being able to mobilize a much higher proportion of the unemployed than it in fact achieved. Particular unemployed workers might more directly have been appealed to in terms of their own values or beliefs (e.g. as Communists), or in terms of a personal obligation (e.g. to the local unemployed committee for successfully preventing eviction or a cut in benefits). But it is difficult to see how unemployed workers, simply because they were unemployed, could have been said to have had a strict moral duty to each other to join the Unemployed Workers Movement. Yet this is precisely the position taken up by many, probably most, trade unionists with respect to union membership.[21]

The reasons for this union attitude are not hard to find. Until forty or fifty years ago trade unions in most industries had to struggle against bitter opposition from employers determined to truck no interference with their right to extract the greatest amount of work for the lowest possible wage. Under these conditions unions assumed for their members the form of instruments

21. It might perhaps be argued that this resulted from the relative lack of authority of the Unemployed Workers Movement compared with the trade unions – a lack of authority stemming from such factors as the Movement's brief existence, the shame attached to being out of work, the shifting composition of the potential membership and low level of active membership, the prominent role of Communists in the organization, and the political nature of the target for attack, i.e. the Government.

of struggle against the poverty, insecurity, degradation and unremitting toil which life constituted for the mass of workers. With unions seen as the instruments of relief, and employers as the instruments of suffering, it is not surprising that trade unionists viewed the non-unionist as at best a dupe or a weakling, at worst a boss's toady or agent. In terms of the working-class conception of solidarity and mutual aid there was no room for declamations of individual rights of self-determination on the issue of unionism. At a different level unions expressed and embodied the interests and needs of all those who worked at a particular trade, protecting their ranks against dilution from workers without, and against undercutting from master's within; thus maintaining both their skills and their wages. It was as natural for craft unions to seek to establish a monopoly right of their members to practise their trade as it was for the Inns of Court in the legal field. Unions of semi-skilled workers, like the miners or cotton spinners, or of unskilled workers, like the seamen or dockers, were on the other hand both more difficult to organize and more vulnerable to the importation of non-union labour. Such union members, faced with employer enmity and worker lethargy, had no time for the rights of the non-unionist, who appeared as an ever-present threat to their livelihood. Union organizers were only too well aware of the difficulties of maintaining membership even in favourable economic conditions – there were always the feckless and the selfish who needed to be persuaded to join or to remain.

The notion that everyone should be left to judge for himself whether or not to join the union was anathema, therefore, to those struggling against employer hostility and greed on the one hand and worker fear or apathy on the other. Unions were built up by stressing the duty of the non-unionist to pay for benefits secured by the union ('your mates are TIRED of carrying you on their backs') and to cease being a hindrance to his fellows ('the non-unionist is a source of danger to other workers').[22] It was

22. The quotations are from organizing leaflets issued in the 1920s – the first by the National Union of Distributive and Allied Workers and the

accepted as axiomatic that the greater the proportion of eligible workers organized, the greater the union's power and authority to act on behalf of the workers in its field. But the most secure and economical way of achieving a high level of membership was to conclude agreements with employers requiring union membership as a *pre-* or *post-*condition of employment, thus forcing men to do what they were seen as being under an obligation to do. As we have seen this is not a recent phenomenon. Skilled workmen in the nineteenth century were accustomed to working in the union (or 'legal') shop under a 'legal' master who observed union conditions regarding pay (the 'list') and apprentices, and who employed only 'legal' men in receipt of union certificates proving their trade competence.[23] As Edward Thompson has stressed, artisans regarded the skill or 'mystery' of their trade 'as their *property*'; and asserted their unquestionable right to the 'quiet and exclusive use and enjoyment of their ... arts and trade'.[24] The establishment of union membership as a condition of employment could be justified in that it provided protection for those who practised the 'mysteries' of their trade and a guarantee to both masters and the public of a high quality product.

This position no longer applies to any significant extent. The closed shop (whether pre-entry or post-entry) as practised today cannot readily be defended, nor is it defended, in these terms; though many employers now see other benefits for *them* in this arrangement.[25] The grounds discussed earlier for asserting a duty

---

second by the National Union of Railwaymen. W. Milne-Bailey (ed.), *Trade Union Documents*, G. Bell & Sons, 1929, pp. 53–4.

23. An interesting discussion of the 'legal' shop is to be found in William Kiddier, *The Old Trade Unions: From Unprinted Records of the Brushmakers*, Ch. 7, 'Legal Men and Legal Shops', George Allen & Unwin, 1930.

24. E. P. Thompson, *The Making of the English Working Class*, Victor Gollancz, 1963; Pelican Books, 1968, p. 279.

25. A survey by the Industrial Relations Research Unit of Warwick University of nearly 1,000 firms with 50 or more employees suggests that 46 per cent of manual and 13 per cent of non-manual workers are covered by the closed shop, and indicates that almost three quarters of managers in these

of all workers to join their appropriate unions are now used as a justification for making union membership a compulsory requirement of employment. As we have seen, the development of collective bargaining, with terms and conditions being negotiated by unions on behalf of the whole workforce, has given rise to strong resentment against 'free-riders', and a determination to use growing union power to end this 'abuse' of the unions by imposing compulsory membership. The denial to a minority of the right to opt out of their moral responsibility to pay for services rendered is seen as an act of justice reached in accordance with the democratic principle of majority rule. But, while in a situation of extreme urgency and necessity it may be justified to force a minority into an association, or to apply association decisions to outsiders, this will apply only where non-association can be shown to constitute a direct and serious threat to the fundamental interests of the majority. In all but the most extreme situations, Article 20(2) of the United Nations Universal Declaration of Human Rights should be adhered to — 'No one may be compelled to belong to an association.'

In his study, *The Closed Shop in Britain*, W. E. J. McCarthy argued that in some trades and industries effective trade union organization amongst the workers was only possible if compulsion were applied, and instanced merchant seamen, musicians, agricultural workers and shop assistants.[26] In many cases, however, closed shop agreements have been concluded in industries where unionization is high and collective bargaining firmly established (as in the mining and railway industries). Nor can one accept the sophistical assertion that closed shop agreements do not compel persons to join unions against their will, since non-unionists are free to refuse to join and to seek other employment. The nineteenth-century restrictions of the right to work through

---

establishments saw advantages in having a closed shop — 'ensures that the union represents all workers', 'helps to stabilize relationships', and 'procedures cover all workers'. Moira Hart, 'Why bosses love the closed shop', *New Society*, 15 February 1979.

26. W. E. J. McCarthy, *The Closed Shop in Britain*, Basil Blackwell, Oxford, 1964.

employer bans against the employment of union members have been replaced by union bans against the employment of non-unionists, although one must recognize their very different social purposes. The former condition was operated by employers to further their economic interests at the expense of the workers, the latter is operated by unions to further the workers' economic interests at the expense of the employer. The former was directed mainly against those who supported the principles and values of trade unionism, the latter against those whose objection is not to trade unionism itself, but to having to pay for sharing in its benefits.

Public concern over the closed shop has primarily and rightly been directed to protecting the right to work of the small minority opposed on grounds of religion or conscience to belonging to a trade union. It should not be assumed, however, that the apathetic, the anti-social and the disillusioned, who constitute the majority of non-unionists, have no valid claim to the right not to 'be compelled to belong to any association'. On the contrary, if rights are to mean anything they must be assertable and exercisable *against* the wishes of the majority, which itself bears the responsibility for demonstrating 'good reasons' why such rights ought not to be exercised in some special circumstances or under some specific conditions. In the nature of things 'good reasons' for social action must always be made in terms of certain values and objectives which are themselves open to question and dispute; although that does not mean that no morally respectable and justifiable case can ever be made for a union-restrictive practice – witness the claims made by nineteenth-century skilled artisans on behalf of the 'legal' shop.

The conclusion of closed shop agreements has important consequences for the union and its members, though it is important to distinguish here between the initial effect when some existing workers are required against their will to join the union rather than be sacked, and that existing when the labour force consists of workers who have chosen to enter closed shop employment. In the initial stage it is questionable whether the 'forced-choice' members can be said to have the same obligations to abide by decisions and respect the rules of the union as 'free' members have. The most one might say is that in choosing membership rather than the sack, they have a quasi-legal obligation to abide by the requirements specifically laid down in the union's rules (e.g. to come out on official strike); but that they cannot be appealed to in terms of the quasi-moral obligations to further the union's purposes and interests (e.g. to take one's turn at picket duty). Some would go further and assert that a 'forced-choice' union member, like a 'forced-choice' religious convert, has no obligations to the organization he is compelled to join. For his part the 'forced-choice' member is unlikely to feel any sense of obligation to the union and, although he may be required to act he will not do so willingly. With a long-established closed shop, as in the newspaper printing industry, one would not expect to find workers with a sense of grievance at having been forced into joining the union; since union membership, like membership of a superannuation scheme or a sports club, will simply be seen as one of the conditions of employment. Workers who might otherwise not have joined the trade union are unlikely to react very differently from the average apathetic union member in carrying out their union responsibilities.

But it does not follow from this that there is no significant difference in the position of the average worker in an established closed shop and in an open shop. The former, unlike the latter, must retain union membership if he is to retain his job. The union man in the closed shop who comes to disagree strongly with his union's policy, or who finds himself in sharp dispute with his local officials, cannot simply drop out of membership. He has to put up with the union: the union does not have to put up with him. Nor can he exercise his right to join or form another association, since closed shop agreements normally provide for membership of specific unions for specified categories of workmen. One ought not to exaggerate the extent or nature of this threat – the number of workers who lose, or who are threatened with the loss of, their jobs as the result of being thrown out of their union is negligible compared with the tens of thousands made redundant by their employers. But it is still valid to question whether extension of closed shop agreements is in the interests of the members of trade unions, in the sense that such arrangements increase the dependence of the members on the organization and the officials, by taking from them the right to 'vote with their feet'. Unions which must be joined and cannot be left might be expected to be more susceptible to oligarchy and arbitrariness, than open trade unions dependent on winning and maintaining their voluntary membership.

Three

The Work Process and Strikes

To understand the nature of the right to strike one must understand the place of strikes in the lives of workers caught up in the industrial work process at the beginning of the nineteenth century. This was the age of entrepreneurial capitalism, the free market society in which each received his due according to the inexorable workings of the laws of supply and demand. The foundation stone of the market society was the free labour market where employer and worker faced each other as buyer and seller respectively. The upshot was a contract of employment, freely entered into, and linking each party to its terms. But those who entered into such contracts were very well aware of their very unequal power positions – inequality which made a mockery of the 'free-bargaining' process. On the one side stood the worker, cap in hand, who must sell his labour in order to eat: on the other the employer seeking extra hands in order to expand his activities and increase his profits. Whereas the capitalist used the labour power he purchased to realize his own ambitions and to express his own will, the industrial worker submitted his will to another, finding outlet for his own personality only after release from his daily toil. The worker was a commodity of production to be used as required and discarded when worn out, injured or redundant.

But the worker was also a human being, with a will of his own, and many rejected the market conception of the model worker as one who devoted himself to his master's interests. The worker as individual might seek to alter or evade the work situation, rather than simply adapt himself to it and be dominated by it. This might

58

be done in a number of ways, which may be gathered under three main headings:

1. Cutting down on the amount of time spent working – absenteeism, malingering, idling, taking unauthorized breaks, bad timekeeping.
2. Exerting some control over the work process – fixing one's own work standards, pace of work, manner of working.
3. Expressions of resentment and dissatisfaction – deliberate bad workmanship or damage to goods, abuse of supervisors, theft.

Each of these activities was commonly engaged in. Each was an end in itself, in that its realization was a direct source of satisfaction or relief; but each had its own limitations and hazards. Each was condemned, not only by employers but by the popular opinion of the age – the first as breaches of faith and contract, the second as usurpations of employer authority, and the third as criminal acts – with each meriting its own particular form of punishment. Nevertheless, workshop idling, pace setting and theft might become so common as to seem almost as practices of the trade – as rights to which workmen were entitled, but which could not be claimed or even publicly admitted to exist.

Thus we have from the beginning a refusal of individuals in the factory situation to abide by the strict theory of the labour contract as a complete alienation of the self to one's master for the contract period. Alongside individual acts of self-assertion and defiance there also emerged modes of collective action which assumed two main forms. The first was informal action devoted to gaining control over the work process, especially the pace of work. Newly employed workers were made aware that they were expected to abide by the norms established by their workmates, not those called for by the employer. The new worker found himself a member of a workshop community which had, to a lesser or greater extent, succeeded in evading or wearing down the full force of employer power over the labour commodity.[1]

1. Peter D. Stearns in his pathbreaking *Lives of Labour: Work in a Maturing Industrial Society*, Croom Helm, 1975, writes '... we know too little

The second form of action was different in that it arose directly out of the formation of trade union and workshop organizations set up for the purpose of negotiating with the employer on behalf of the workforce. To back up their demands these organizations used a wide range of weapons of persuasion, of which the following were the most important:

1. Strike.
2. 'Go-slow'.
3. Work to rule (strict and painstaking adherence to all the detailed rules of the trade or workshop).
4. Overtime ban.
5. Withdrawal of cooperation with management.
6. Taking over the factory.
7. Organized sabotage.

The seventh has rarely been used, and even less rarely advocated in Britain, though it was strongly espoused in some syndicalist circles at the beginning of the century. Where sabotage occurs it is normally in the context of a bitter industrial dispute and is carried out by individual strikers, without the authority of the strike organizers. Factory take-overs are a recent reaction to factory shut-downs and large-scale redundancy. They have recently gained the blessing of the British Trades Union Congress as 'an appropriate union tactic' . . . 'to limit the rights of owners and managers of capital to take action detrimental to large groups of work people', even though 'technically illegal'.[2]

The remaining forms of action are all well-established methods of union and workshop struggle and all of them are legal in Britain; though the fifth presupposes an advanced stage of union-

---

about the collective action most directly related to work, the effort to keep production down in order to protect both jobs and an appropriate rhythm of work. This was not necessarily protest at all, in that it followed from a widely-shared view that there were appropriate limits to stress and to output' (p. 300).

2. *Industrial Democracy: Report of the T.U.C. General Council to the 1974 Trades Union Congress*, p. 31.

management relationships which existed in few industries before the Second World War. The strike and the 'go-slow' were proscribed together and legalized together, but banning overtime and working to rule could not readily be made illegal without violating the notion of the free labour contract. What is interesting to note is that none of the other traditional methods of union struggle has ever attained the status of the strike weapon, either for unionists or the public at large. In large part this no doubt reflects the greater dramatic and wounding impact of the strike over other union weapons, but in some measure it is also a reflection of the greater moral strength of the case for the strike weapon in a free market society. Striking was the action of a free man who quit work, lost pay and risked losing his job for a cause he believed in: going slow was the action of dishonest men who sought to draw full pay for half-work or less. In terms of the prevailing free market principles you could not have a justified 'go-slow', since the 'go-slow' weapon was inherently deceitful and underhand.

So far, striking has been looked at as:

1. A means of putting pressure on employers to secure the remedy of some known grievance or the grant of some stated demand.

This is a conception of striking which fits readily into the rational choice picture of industrial relations as collective bargaining conducted by parties each concerned with the protection of its own interests and the realization of its own ends. But striking may be understood in a number of other ways, as:

2. A means of making an employer aware of some grievance.
3. An expression of frustration or dissatisfaction.
4. A denial of managerial authority.
5. An interruption of the work process.
6. A rest from working.

These different understandings of what a strike *is* are not, of course, mutually exclusive. Indeed one might assert that a strike necessarily involves an interruption of the work process (5) and provides a rest from working (6); that it always arises out of, and gives expression to some frustration or dissatisfaction (3); that it is bound to alert management to the existence of some grievance (2); and that it is always, if only implicitly, a denial of managerial authority (4). The only feature which may be lacking is the expression of specific demands or grievances (1), since these often emerge only during the course of a dispute.[3] But it is precisely the stated demand or grievance which constitutes the foundation for the rational choice model of collective bargaining.

At this point it is pertinent to ask what industrial sociology has to tell us about the nature and role of strikes in the work situation. Broadly speaking we may distinguish two main currents of thought – the first sees industrial society as a social unity with common interests and values, the second sees it as a coalition of groups with conflicting interests and competing values. On the first view strikes are dysfunctional, destructive of the industrial social fabric, non-rational responses to the work situation indicative of ignorance, prejudice or the presence of alien influences and values. In these terms there is no place for any conception of a moral right to strike for any purpose, but this does not mean that strikes ought to be legally forbidden. They should rather be regarded as symptoms of industrial sickness requiring appropriate managerial treatment.

The second, or pluralist view, is much nearer in approach to that of most of those engaged in collective bargaining. Workers are recognized as having different interests from their employer; interests which they are entitled to press by a variety of means, including strikes. Strikes, that is to say, can be seen as rational and legitimate responses by workers when used 'as a means of putting pressure on employers to remedy some known grievance or grant some stated demand'. Strikes may also serve to make employers aware of some grievance, to give expression to frustration or dissatisfaction, to exemplify a denial of managerial

3. Tony Lane and Kenneth Roberts in *Strike at Pilkingtons*, Fontana, 1971, have stressed that in spontaneous walk-outs or 'wild-cat' strikes, 'It is by no means unusual for the demands to be formulated *after* the strike has started' (p.17).

authority, or a desire to shut down the work process which governs the worker's life, and to escape from the factory. These further ends may be served by strikes for workers in modern industrial society, but they are not seen by industrial pluralism as legitimate ends for strikers themselves directly to pursue, although they may reasonably derive indirect satisfaction or benefit from their realization as a result of pursuing a strike demand.

What makes these functional ends served *by* strikers unacceptable as ends *for* strikers are the values assumed and embodied in the industrial pluralist approach. As Alan Fox has put it, 'The assumption is being made that while conflicts arise over the terms of economic collaboration, values and norms are not so divergent that workable compromises cannot be achieved. Underlying the cut and thrust of market place and organizational encounters ... lies the rock-firm foundation of a stable and agreed social system ... In order to maintain that system they submit to compromise and find themselves able, for this purpose, to share moral beliefs which teach the importance of observing agreements freely and honourably undertaken.'[4] Strikes undertaken to express resentment, to interrupt the work process, to make life difficult for management or to get a few days extra holiday demonstrate all too clearly the absence of any shared values or norms of behaviour. Striking is regarded as dysfunctional by industrial pluralists when it conflicts with the terms and interests of the free collective bargaining system of which, on this view, it is a part. Workers are, therefore, only justified in exercising the right to strike within the rules and understandings of the industrial bargaining game as played between unions and management.

The industrial pluralist approach is particularly important since it accords closely with the positions taken up by trade union leaders both in Britain and North America. There is, perhaps, nothing very surprising about this, since experience indicates that participation in industrial collective bargaining serves to promote respect for the rules and institutions of the bargaining game

4. Alan Fox, 'Industrial Relations: A Social Critique of Plurist Ideology', in J. Child (ed.), *Man and Organization*, Allen & Unwin, 1973, pp. 197–8.

as serving the broad common purposes of the players. The maintenance of the practice of collective bargaining comes to have for both parties priority over unqualified furtherance of sectional interest, in the sense that neither the demands made, nor the methods employed, may be such as to subvert the practice itself. This is the industrial equivalent of the practice of British parliamentary government which requires that the ruling party's policies are kept within the limits of what the opposition party can tolerate.

The pluralist appraisal of strikes as a constituent of the union-employer practice of collective bargaining is open to challenge by those who do not accept the values and assumptions embodied in that approach. Thus for the alienated apathetic worker, work is but a form of forced labour from which any escape is welcome. Strikes provide just such a respite, plus the satisfaction which can be derived from 'buggering-up the works'. Appeals from any quarter for the worker to take up a responsible attitude to his job, to improve output and efficiency, to refrain from 'wild-cat' strikes and abide by collective bargaining procedures fall on his deaf ears, since he refuses to recognize any common interest with, or to accept any moral obligation to, those who employ him. A similar, but more firmly grounded and articulated view, underlies the position of the Marxist. Although the Marxist will sympathize with the attitude and sentiments of the alienated worker, he will want to harness this resentment to more direct and positive ends. While, for the Marxist, strikes may legitimately express workers' frustration, deny managerial authority, interrupt the work process or provide a break from working, these can never be adequate ends in themselves. Such sentiments need rather to be worked on and harnessed to specific strike demands, formulated and fought for, so that workers may come to see themselves as members of an exploited class engaged in battle with their class enemy, instead of as embittered individuals merely concerned with reducing their own personal alienation experience.

Richard Hyman, a leading Marxist writer on industrial relations, has developed the following critique of the role of strikes within the present practice of collective bargaining:

> Since managerial control is legitimized in our culture, it is not surprising that acceptance of a wide area of managerial prerogative is one of the foundations of collective bargaining. Workers, too, cannot formulate explicitly those grievances which stem from the exercise of managerial control without questioning their very subjection to this control. The basic necessity that every strike must be settled means, moreover, that workers are obliged to specify their grievances in a form which permits resolution *in negotiation with employers*. Where workers' deprivations derive from their very status as employees, the requirements of the strike situation prevent this grievance from receiving articulation.[5]

Hyman's thesis is a fertile one. It helps to explain how employer acceptance of collective bargaining has altered the form of workers' grievances which have now to meet the requirements of legitimacy embodied in the bargaining practice and be processable through that practice. It also serves to account for the unwillingness, or inability, of trade unions and their members publicly to claim a right to strike except in respect of stated grievances or demands of the kind dealt with by the normal negotiating machinery. Workers no longer talk of strikes as 'holidays' and striking as 'playing' as they did in the nineteenth century, when negotiating machinery as we know it did not exist. At that time, when the legal right to strike was severely circumscribed and the moral legitimacy of unions and strikes widely disputed by employers, it was possible, as Hyman points out, for the rest from work inherent in striking to be 'explicitly valued for its own sake'.[6]

During the past forty years two parallel and related developments have taken place in the position of the British working

5. Richard Hyman, *Strikes*, Fontana, 1972, p. 124.
6. ibid., p. 132.

class. One has been the experience, until very recently at least, of continuous low levels of unemployment and rising living standards, which created *for the first time* amongst ordinary workers a belief in and expectation of economic progress *for them* within the existing social and economic order. The other has been a radical change in the position of trade unions: their recognition by virtually all employers, their participation in a complex network of industrial bargaining processes, and their involvement in a wide range of Government economic and social policy-making. These twin developments go a long way to explain the shift in the basic character of most strikes noted by both Charles Tilly and Peter Stearns, from backward-looking and defensive to forward-looking and assertive.[7]

What has not been noted is that the conditions which helped bring about this shift have made it increasingly difficult for trade unions to countenance strike action in furtherance of what are popularly seen as economically backward causes. As anxious and willing participants in a neo-capitalist society they cannot rationally assert a right to strike against measures for maintaining and improving the efficiency of the very enterprises on which their members' present well-being and future expectations are seen to depend. Unions find it difficult to resist the *principle* of rationalization and mechanization of the work process and consequently must confine themselves to negotiating the terms and conditions of its introduction; though the price they are able to exact may be a high one, as in the long drawn-out dispute at Times Newspapers. Trade union leaders consciously seek to confine strikes within the collective bargaining system and to purposes appropriate to that system. The workers on the shop floor, too, find it difficult to resist this tendency to turn all workshop or trade *principles* into *objects* of bargaining, which one should be prepared to trade at their market-value – whether the principles

7. Charles Tilly, 'Collective Violence in European Perspective', in H. D. Graham and T. D. Gurr (eds.), *The History of Violence in America: Historical and Comparative Perspectives*, F. A. Praeger, New York, 1969. Peter N. Stearns, *International Review of Social History*, 1974.

concern established trade practices, manning levels, pace of work, downgrading of job skills or redundancy. The right to strike has increasingly come to be seen, accepted and asserted as a tool to be used in a bargaining process which resolves all disputes and grievances into disputes and grievances about money.

But is the right to strike in Western societies nothing more than a right possessed by relatively prosperous workers to use a particularly effective tool in the collective bargaining procedures of neo-capitalism to improve their position still further? In 1968 Professor B. C. Roberts, then head of the department of trade union studies at the London School of Economics, strongly urged this view when he wrote:

> The strike under modern conditions is a much more effective weapon when used by those who are already well-off and wish to be even better off ... those at the bottom of the social pyramid very rarely succeed in improving their relative status by this means ... It is hard to justify a strike of relatively well-paid employees for higher incomes in money terms, when the costs of the strike are paid by the community in terms of goods or services, higher prices, and possibly higher taxes, especially since the poorest members of the community will have no means of protecting themselves against these costs. On any kind of utilitarian calculus, based upon a cost benefit analysis, it is the weakest that go to the wall and the strong that gain by strike action.[8]

Professor Roberts attacks the strike weapon because it works to the benefit of the strong rather than the weak, but he fails to recognize that it was precisely because the free market society was found by bitter experience to be one in which the rewards went to the economically privileged and powerful, that the weak at the wall combined together and armed themselves with the strike weapon in the first place. But while combination was an

8. B. C. Roberts (ed.), *Industrial Relations: Contemporary Issues. First World Congress of the International Industrial Relations Association, Geneva, 1967*, Macmillan, 1968, Introduction, pp. xxi–xxii.

instrument of self-help for groups of workers in separate trades with varying powers and interests, there was always an underlying sense of belonging to a wider movement with broader common aims. This first found full expression in the rules of the Grand National Consolidated Trades Union of Great Britain and Ireland (1834), 'whose great and ultimate object must be to establish the paramount rights of Industry and Humanity, by instituting such measures as shall effectually prevent the ignorant, idle and useless part of Society from having that undue control over the fruits of our toil, which ... they at present possess'.[9] Trade unions have been concerned to use their power and influence (of which the strike weapon is a vital constituent), not only to secure better pay and conditions for their own members, but to realize improvements in the economic and social position of the whole working class. Far from these wider objectives being a minor or separate concern of trade unions, unrelated to the bread and butter issues pursued through collective bargaining, they have served to enlighten and widen that process.

At the beginning of this chapter it was argued that individual factory workers, instead of adapting to, and being dominated by, the work situation might seek to alter or evade it in three ways:

1. Cutting down the amount of time spent working.
2. Exerting some control over the work process.
3. Expressing resentment and dissatisfaction.

But while such action carried with it the danger of dismissal, trade unions might hope to realize the inherent purposes through negotiation. Thus it has always been a major union objective to cut down work time through reductions in the working week and the institution of paid holidays. Exercising control over the work

9. *Rules and Regulations of the Grand National Consolidated Trades Union of Great Britain and Ireland, Instituted for the Purpose of More Effectually Enabling the Working Classes to Secure, Protect, and Establish the Rights of Industry*, 1834, quoted in Sidney and Beatrice Webb, *The History of Trade Unionism 1666–1920*, printed by the authors for the Trade Unionists of the United Kingdom, Christmas 1919, Appendix II.

process, though still in part realized conventionally and unofficially within the workshop community, has increasingly become the object of union action; and while the essential nature of the employer-worker relationship has not changed, both the concept and the practice of managerial sovereignty have been seriously eroded. Modern managers and foremen need to secure, and expect to have to secure, at least the acquiescence of those they no longer command as of established right and power. The worker in a union shop is no longer at the mercy of an almighty master ruling an industrial kingdom with a mixture of paternalism and despotism. Unions have also helped to create machinery through which workers may seek redress of some of the griev-ances which underlie their resentments and dissatisfactions.

INDUSTRIAL DEMOCRACY

In recent years there has been increasing consensus among trade unions on the need to greatly extend the scope of collective bar-gaining to include a whole range of questions traditionally ac-cepted as being exclusively of managerial concern: decisions about 'production programming, workshop layout and the tech-nology and design of plant and machinery' and 'major decisions on investment, location, closures, take-overs and mergers, and product specializaton'.[10] *The Bullock Report on Industrial Democracy* (1977) expressed its own conviction, as follows:

> The problem of Britain as an industrialized nation is not a lack of native capacity in its working population so much as a fai-lure to draw out their energies and skill to anything like their full potential. It is our belief that the way to release those energies, to provide greater satisfaction in the workplace and to assist in raising the level of productivity and efficiency in British in-dustry – and with it the living standards of the nation – is not by recrimination or exhortation but by putting the relationship between capital and labour on to a new basis which will involve

10. Trades Union Congress, *Industrial Democracy*, T.U.C., 1974, pp. 29 and 35.

not just management but the whole workforce in sharing responsibility for the success and profitability of the enterprise. Such a change in the industrial outlook and atmosphere will only come about, however, as a result of giving the representatives of the employees a real, and not a sham or token, share in making the strategic decisions about the future of an enterprise which in the past have been reserved to management and the representatives of the shareholders.[11]

How might such a transformation of union collective bargaining into union participatory management be viewed in terms of the different moral approaches outlined in Chapter 1, and what impact might it be expected to have on their appraisals of the right to strike? Strong support for the implementation of industrial democracy can be inferred from the principles of natural justice and Rawlsian justice. The natural justice tradition is entirely in sympathy with the tenor of the Bullock Report, offering as it does the prospect of a replacement of the principles of political economy by those of moral economy, and of industrial conflict by industrial cooperation. In such a context the 'last resort' use of the strike weapon could be justified less and less frequently. If industrial democracy works as its sponsors claim the result should be the withering away of the strike. The prospect of a radical shift in worker-employer relations towards greater equality of power is one which fits in particularly well with the Rawlsian conception of justice. Rawlsians would be concerned, however, to ensure that industrial democracy did not result in benefits for the vested minority of organized labour and capital at the expense of the weakest members of the community.

Serious reservations regarding industrial democracy could be expected from two opposite quarters – the individualists and the Marxists. Economic individualism is bitterly opposed to any further eroding of master and managerial rights and prerogatives, whether stemming from union pressure or a misguided belief in

11. *Report of the Committee of Inquiry on Industrial Democracy* (Chairman, Lord Bullock), H.M.S.O., 1977, p. 160.

co-partnership. Union power is directed both to subverting the right of the employer to employ his capital as he thinks fit, and to depriving him of the fruits of his investment. The institution of collective bargaining throughout industry has increased the incidence and severity of industrial conflict; its extension through industrial democracy will increase the range of issues over which conflict arises, while making it much more difficult for managements, uncertain about their role and position, to mount a firm response. The likely outcome is industrial chaos. Nozick's stance is similar but based on more fundamental objections, since he rejects outright the underlying principle of industrial democracy 'that people have a right to a say in the decisions that importantly affect their lives'. This he does on the grounds that 'after we exclude from consideration the decisions which others have a right to make, and the actions which would . . . violate *my* rights, it is not clear there are *any* decisions remaining about which even to raise the question of whether I have a right to a say in those that importantly affect me. Certainly if there are any left to speak about, they are not significant enough a portion to provide a case for a different sort of State'; i.e. a 'non-minimal' State with power to enforce such a right to a say.[12] Industrial democracy, like collective bargaining, should be an entirely voluntary activity undertaken only where both parties expect to benefit.

The Marxist approach to industrial democracy is ambivalent. On the one hand it might provide a means for fighting the class struggle in a new way by giving workers' representatives a foothold within the managerial citadel, opening up the prospect of fighting for workers' control of the factories and the revolutionary perspective of a workers' takeover. On the other hand, industrial democracy might all too easily become a device for inveigling workers' representatives into the processes of capitalist management, into the organization, that is, of their own exploitation. To secure the one and prevent the other a high degree of industrial militancy, and a greater readiness to use the strike weapon, would

12. Robert Nozick, *Anarchy, State, and Utopia*, Basil Blackwell, Oxford, 1974, pp. 268–70.

be required. In a less ideological form these differing concerns are shared by many active trade unionists. Union militants favouring industrial democracy see it as a means of extracting concessions and benefits for their members by putting a price on each and every item of agreement, while avoiding responsibility for unpalatable decisions likely to arouse worker opposition. Their opponents fear that industrial democracy will result in unions wasting their time on matters of no direct concern to their members, and to their being forced to assume responsibility for 'selling' to those members unpopular managerial decisions.

The moral realist might be expected to accept that each of these union expectations would be realized under different conditions in different plants. Whether unions would be wise to press for the extension of collective bargaining into new areas of decision-making is questionable. Certainly the moral realist would see no reason to accept the Bullock report's optimistic assessment that industrial democracy will promote productivity and efficiency, quite possibly the reverse. In the short to medium run there appear little or no grounds for the assumption that industrial democracy will reduce industrial tension and the level of strike activity. The only effective way of doing that is to find ways of cutting back the power and influence of union representatives on the shop floor.

Four

Employers and Strikes

Until well into the second half of the nineteenth century the dominant approach of the employing class to trade unions and strikes was, as we have seen, one of firm opposition. The force of that opposition stemmed in large part from employer conviction that right and reason, in the form of the principles of political economy, were on their side. Economic individualism asserted the moral right of each employer to run his own business as he thought fit, and his moral duty to resist encroachment by trade unions on employer prerogatives and practices. Only in this way could one preserve the free competitive market system on which the well-being and liberty of all depended. This moral philosophy engendered a crusading spirit against combinations and strikes amongst employers; a spirit which was inflamed by the violence and coercion associated in the public mind with early trade unionism.

With the growth of 'responsible' unionism in the years of Victorian prosperity, and with increasing concern within society about the position and problems of the working classes, the sovereignty of the principles of political economy, as practised by class-confident employers, was increasingly challenged in the name of Christian humanity and the principles of natural justice. Trade unions were held to have a positive role to play in protecting the legitimate interests of workers. Such interests were not incompatible with the legitimate interests of employers, but they were incompatible with the conception of hired labour as a commodity to be used by the employer as he willed, subject only to the terms of the contract of hire. Employers should recognize

73

the right of trade unions to speak and act on behalf of their members, and seek to establish a working relationship with them.

In these terms it was the responsibility of both employers and unions to avoid industrial conflict; and, if on occasion conflict arose, each party should seek to resolve the differences and restore harmony as soon as possible. While this might well require employer resistance to what was seen as unjustified and unreasonable union demands, it precluded treating strikes as industrial wars and strikers as an enemy to be beaten into submission. Employers should avoid methods of resisting strike action, such as the importation of strike-breaking labour, which inflamed worker hostility by threatening their livelihood, or which, like eviction from company houses, imposed unnecessary and unwarranted hardship on strikers' wives and families. Even on narrow utilitarian grounds of self-interest it could be argued that employers should be sparing in using their extensive legal rights of strike-combat. To defeat their striking workers by all-out warfare, as the coal-owners defeated successive miners' strikes, was simply to fertilize the seeds for further bitter disputes. Even where employers were morally as well as legally entitled to act, e.g. to dismiss strikers who were in breach of contract, wider considerations of both morality and self-interest might suggest restraint, to facilitate an amicable solution of the dispute. Such considerations as these might be still more strongly urged where an employer initiated conflict through a lock-out or the introduction of the 'document'. The lock-out, like the strike, ought to be a last resort weapon, while the use of the 'document' was morally unacceptable since it effectively deprived individual workers of their legal and moral right to act in association.

As the groundswell of public opinion in favour of employers adopting a more positive and less belligerent attitude to trade unions grew, employers gradually came to doubt the validity of the role of industrial Leviathans cast for them by economic individualism. Though the development was uneven as between different employers and different trades (the mine-owners remained committed to fighting the unions until their final demise in 1947), the general direction was clear. This change in employer attitudes was furthered by, and itself furthered, three other changes in the industrial area which became increasingly important after 1939.

1. The concentration of capital and employment and the displacement of masters by managers.
2. The growth of a comprehensive system of collective bargaining at national and workshop level.
3. A great increase in trade union membership and the building up of strong shop steward and workshop organizations in most large industrial enterprises.

The days of the assertive entrepreneur, fully confident in himself and in the social value of his calling, have steadily faded from present view into past history. The person of the master of industry, responsible only to himself and entitled to indulge his principles or whims even at risk to *his* business, has been superseded by corporate management, responsible to the company's shareholders for its stewardship. The present-day managers of huge bureaucratized enterprises have neither the incentives nor the opportunities to stamp their indelible mark on the face of industry. They do not respond to strikes as a personal challenge to their authority and are more concerned with maintaining a favourable public image as 'responsible' employers, than in breaking their opponents by any means legally permitted.

The emergence of collective bargaining between employers and unions has had a more profound impact on managerial attitudes to industrial relations than on union and worker attitudes. Collective bargaining has become an integral part of the managerial process, directed to the resolution of problems through discussion and compromise. The power of management is seen to lie in its ability to refuse to accede to union demands or make further concessions; leaving it to the union side to determine whether or not to initiate industrial action.

This is in marked contrast to the nineteenth century when employer associations made extensive use of lock-outs; even on occasion going so far as to impose secondary lock-outs on firms whose workers had already accepted the association's terms in order to help break the resistance of workers in those factories who stood out against them. The first national conference of trade union delegates held in Sheffield in 1866 was called to discuss the growing threat of lock-outs: a threat which it was hoped might be abated by building up out-of-work funds on the one hand and discouraging strikes on the other.[1] The lock-out remained a prominent feature of the British industrial scene right down to the 1920s, especially in the mining and engineering unions; but has since wasted away through neglect. The great mass of employers have unilaterally come to abandon the lock-out in the face of unions still committed to the strike weapon. How is this anomaly to be explained? The obvious answer which suggests itself is that unions have grown so powerful that it no longer makes sense for firms to initiate or aggravate an industrial confrontation which they cannot expect to win as they could fifty or more years ago. But, important as this factor is, it takes no account of the differences in the nature of lock-outs and strikes, differences which have been masked by their acceptance as equivalents in both law and popular thinking. Even George Odger, the radical Secretary of the London Trades Council, expressed in 1866 his readiness to 'accept lock-outs as a legitimate result of strikes'.[2]

But the lock-out was not simply a weapon to be used by employers to force unions to accept wage reductions or withdraw wage demands; it was an anti-union weapon. Many nineteenth-century employers resorted to the lock-out with the deliberate intention of breaking up the unions, and even where there was no such intention the inevitable consequence of a successful lock-out was a severe weakening of union influence and membership. The strike is not an anti-employer weapon in the same sense. It is not

1. See *Trades' Societies and Lock-Outs: Report of the Conference of Trades Delegates of the United Kingdom held in Sheffield on July 17–21, 1866,* Lawley Bros., Sheffield.
2. ibid.

designed, even in the eyes of Marxists, as a means for breaking the power of the employer but for extracting concessions from him. Indeed, one of the strongest arguments that an employer can deploy against a wage claim is that its concession would put him out of business. It is not the force of this argument which unions doubt but its truth. The strike, but not the lock-out, could be incorporated into the system of collective bargaining; since, while the former could be accepted as a 'last resort' weapon by the employers, the latter could not be so accepted by the unions.

Essentially the same situation exists with respect to the other powerful weapons legally available to employers in a strike situation – the threat of the 'document' or the importation of strike-breakers. No union could possibly accept the right of employers to use such anti-union instruments. The development of comprehensive collective bargaining has consequently come to require the forfeiture by employers of these weapons along with the lock-out. It is only in the smaller firm, where the level of union membership and the sense of worker solidarity are low, that there are still to be found employers and managers ready to utilize their legal rights to do battle with the unions with a view to beating them. This is most likely to occur, as in the 1976–7 dispute at Grunwick, where the issue is one of union recognition, since recognition involves the acceptance of collective bargaining procedures which deny the validity of employer counter-strike warfare. The Grunwick dispute revealed the extent to which trade union power is dependent for its effectiveness on securing collective bargaining recognition; for the whole weight of the trade union movement (including the sustained use of mass picketing) was inadequate to force this small firm to recognize the union.

Today's employers have not only lost the power unilaterally to determine the wages and conditions of their employees, but have renounced their right to respond aggressively to union strike attack. They have been locked into a system of collective bargaining which is expected by today's trade union leaders and members to provide regular increases in real income each year, irrespective of levels of productivity, of employment, or the terms of trade. These expectations have become for employers part of the *facts* of the British industrial scene, so that even in recession there is no longer any question of cutting wages or refusing an increase but only of finding the minimum figure at which the union side will be prepared to settle. If no agreement can be reached then the outcome is never a lock-out but a strike, which may be lost by the workers but which cannot be won by the employers, since they are unable to take steps to beat the union and unilaterally impose their own terms and conditions. Today's employers are expected, and expect, to continue to negotiate with union representatives during a stoppage until they come up with a sufficiently improved offer to persuade the unions to call on their members to return to work.

Where a strike is completely solid there is nothing that a present-day employer can do other than to shut down his plant and to pick an operative time to re-open negotiations. He cannot rely, as latter-day masters did, on mounting hunger and family suffering driving his workmen to break off the strike, since the modern State provides for the basic needs of strikers and their families. He has no way of putting pressure on the strikers themselves; though he may seek to influence them by circulating details of the employer's case and offer.

The situation is rather different where, as more commonly occurs, the employer is faced with a partial strike, where only some of the workers in a factory take strike action, or where only some groups of workers are in dispute. Each of these situations offers the possibility of keeping the factory open and partially operative; thus reducing the economic impact of the strike, and increasing the prospect of securing an earlier and a more favourable settlement with the striking union. The most difficult problems are raised by 'blacklegs' who refuse to join the strike. Such men may be seen as workers who have remained loyal to the firm and who, by their loyalty, have established a right to employer protection and support in working. But the exercise of the legal right not to strike is the exercise of an *immunity* right against one's fellow workers and does not establish a *claim* right against one's employer to provide both work and protection. 'Black-legging' is an act of disloyalty to one's striking colleagues, but that does not make it a positive act of loyalty to the employer, imposing on him a duty to provide work and protection, especially since the 'blackleg's' motives are likely to be entirely self-interested. The most that might be argued is that an employer has a moral right to decide whether to continue to provide work for those who exercise their legal right not to strike and a moral duty to secure protection for those he does employ. But if he exercises that right he is liable to engender bitterness amongst the striking unionists, which will, unless the strike is very weakly supported, strongly militate against the prospect of an early and satisfactory settlement.

Rather different but still more tricky problems are raised if the strike is confined to some sections only of the workforce. Unions have traditionally adopted the position that the members of a union not in dispute ought not to carry out any of the work normally done by members of another union in dispute with the same employer. Attempts by an employer to force a breach of this fundamental principle of union solidarity would be bound to meet with strong resistance and possibly lead to strike action. Where an employer is faced with a protracted strike of one section of his workforce he is likely to see the situation as one in which he is 'forced' to lay off other groups of workers, since it does not make economic sense to carry on production. Such lay-offs may also be designed to generate pressure from a non-striking union on to the striking union to come to a quick settlement. Where an employer is successful in keeping his partially 'struck' factory working his very success may generate tougher action by those on strike; in particular action to prevent goods entering and leaving the factory. It is a cardinal principle of worker solidarity not to cross other strikers' picket lines and, as long as only peaceful persuasion is used, the employer has neither a right of legal redress nor a power of counter-attack. He is even more powerless to prevent his strikers taking secondary picket action against his main suppliers and customers, although such suppliers and customers may themselves apply for legal injunctions against the pickets.

Though an employer must seek to negotiate the best settlement he can to extricate himself from a costly strike situation, he may be able to take preventive action against future hurtful stoppages. The remedy which most readily suggests itself to the employer's mind is to find some pretext for dismissing the militants who led the strike struggle. The operation requires careful handling, or else it may rebound and precipitate a further bitter dispute, since the protection of strike leaders against victimization is recognized as a fundamental obligation of, and a fundamental condition for, effective trade unionism. Alternatively an employer may seek to conclude 'no strike' agreements with the trade unions or 'last resort' strike agreements, specifying the conditions in which strike action may be resorted to. Both types of agreement are commonly to be found in the United States, usually in association with arbitration provisions, but the evidence suggests that such agreements have had only limited effect in reducing the level of unofficial and unconstitutional strikes[3]. It is, of course, precisely such strikes, many of brief duration and often involving only relatively few workers, which comprise the great bulk of stoppages in Britain and which cause the greatest disruption in British industry. It is precisely such strikes which neither employers nor unions are able to prevent and which they find most difficult to settle. The level of unofficial and unconstitutional strikes is from the employers' angle a serious limitation to collective bargaining, stemming from the unions' inability to secure their members' adherence to agreements made.

From the traditional employer standpoint the industrial bargaining scene presents a sorry picture. Having traded in their weapons of industrial warfare to secure industrial peace through

3. See Jack Steiber, 'Grievance Arbitration in the United States: An Analysis of its Effects and Functions', *Royal Commission on Trade Unions and Employers' Associations, Research Papers 8*, H.M.S.O., 1968. Steiber investigated 757 'no strike' and 780 'limited strike' agreements in the United States.

collective bargaining, employers, when faced with unacceptable union demands, find themselves forced to rely on negotiating with strike-armed official union forces, while uncontrolled union guerrilla forces are able to strike at will. The economic individualist would find much to lament but nothing to surprise him in this assessment. Employers are the authors of their own misfortunes. Lamely they have not only conceded to the unions a right of interference in their affairs but have abandoned the very weapons necessary to protect their interests against growing union encroachment. Though the odds are now strongly weighted against employers, the only way to prevent the loss of such authority and power as remains to them is to reassert employer rights. Employers should seek to curb the power of the trade unions, instead of cooperating with the unions in curbing their own. While it would be foolish, in the face of much more powerful union forces, to adopt the attitudes and methods of tough-minded nineteenth-century employers, today's employers should take up as forceful and uncompromising an approach to unions as circumstances permit. Employers should be ready to use their legal rights of lock-out, to deal with widespread unofficial disruption, and to dismiss and replace workers involved in unofficial strike action. In particular employers should cease to cooperate with unions in spreading the closed shop. Nothing is more objectionable in economic individualist eyes than the sight of employers exercising *their* right to hire whom *they* please, to hire only those whom it pleases the *union* to have hired.

Nozick's historical entitlement theory, in rejecting that any person or group has a moral claim to a just share in a society's economic and social goods based on merit, need, output or effort, substantiates the right of property rights holders, like employers, to maintain those rights against encroachment.[4] While employers might voluntarily agree to give up some of their proprietorial rights to the unions, they ought not to be compulsorily deprived of rights, like the right of dismissal, to benefit either their

4. See Robert Nozick, *Anarchy, State, and Utopia*, Basil Blackwell, Oxford, 1974, Ch. 7, 'Distributive Justice', Section 1.

employees or society at large, without the payment of compensation. Where rights are surrendered in voluntary exchange, as with a commitment to voluntary collective bargaining, employers are entitled to strict observance by the unions of the terms of the bargain made. If the unions are unwilling or unable to abide by those terms, then the employer is absolved from any obligation. Thus, if unions fail to comply with disputes procedures and take industrial action, or if a strike is called by workers in spite of official union opposition, employers are entitled to take such steps as they feel necessary to protect their interests; including the withdrawal of union recognition and the replacement of striking union labour by non-union labour. Since the upholding of entitled rights and of voluntary exchange is the basis of a free society, the Law and the Courts ought to uphold the sanctity of free contracts and provide compensation for the violation of labour contracts or for injuries suffered by employers through industrial action. The privileged legal position of trade unions should be removed – employers should be entitled to sue trade unions for damages caused by strike action, and the picketing of firms not involved in a trades dispute should be forbidden.

The Marxist might, in contrast, be expected to argue that employers, as employers, had no moral rights; particularly no moral rights against workers in industrial disputes. But while Marxists might claim that employers had no moral right to lock out their workers, to dismiss strikers or to employ substitute labour, and that they should be deprived of their legal right so to act, it does not follow that a Marxist would deny *all* legal rights to employers. Marxists are required by the nature of their value system to accept that employers may reasonably claim rights in terms of their role in, and the values of, capitalist society: roles and values which are historically validated for Marxists as preparing the way for the realization of socialism. It might even be argued, with Georges Sorel[5], that by asserting and giving effect to their right relentlessly to fight strikes, employers sharpen class conflict and heighten class consciousness, thereby hastening

5. See Georges Sorel, *Reflections on Violence*, 1908.

their own overthrow. Strikes in capitalist society derive from the fundamental fact that employers control workers' access to the means of production. However powerful trade unions may become under capitalism, they cannot, Marxists argue, fundamentally alter the nature of that dependent relationship on capital. The right of workers to strike, therefore, presupposes the right of capitalists to resist and refuse worker demands. Employer resistance compels workers to choose between acceptance of his terms and strike action. While strikers may be able, by a combination of worker power and legal enactment, to secure protection of their jobs when striking, they can never protect themselves against the risk of defeat. Employers may lose the legal right to fight strikes by certain methods, but they necessarily retain as a minimum a right to refuse striker demands, and, in the last resort, to close down their factories.

In Marxist terms employer rights rest on a power position rather than a rights foundation, and the same is true for the moral realist approach; though it lacks any preconception of, or commitment to, any particular historical outcome to industrial development. In realist terms it is not the morality of strike-breaking that is at issue but the cost and effect. While it may pay Grunwick to fight a strike for union recognition by busing-in blackleg labour, it is not open to Fords or Shell to do so. It is the power of the unions and the established system of collective bargaining in large enterprises which, on this view, rules out employer resort to lock-outs and strike-breaking, not employer or public doubts as to their morality. Employers have to make the best they can of their present depressed position in relation to the trade unions, taking advantage of current changes of political government and economic climate to secure such improvements as they may be able to wrest.

More positive, but still critical, responses to the conception of employer rights are to be found in the principles of natural justice and of Rawlsian justice. Natural justice, as we have seen, rejects the whole conception of the inherent right of employers, in defence of the sovereign rights of proprietorship, to use any weapon not legally proscribed to impose their will on striking workers. But in championing the rights of workers, natural justice upholds the rights of the good employer and the duties of the good workman. Employers are thus entitled to resist the attempts of unions to secure unreasonable or unjust demands under threat of strike action; especially when the unions concerned are unwilling to submit the matter in dispute to arbitration. Faced with the prospect of the continuation of widespread and persistent industrial action, disruptive of the whole work process, an employer might, 'as a last resort', lock out the workforce or dismiss the instigators of the disruption. Similarly there would be no objection in principle to an employer dismissing workers taking unwarranted strike action. But such a response could be justified in terms of natural justice only where persistent attempts to secure redress of legitimate employer grievances against workers and unions through the normal negotiating channels had failed, and where the economic prospects for the firm of a continuance of current levels of unrest were serious.

The Rawlsian approach to justice is somewhat different, concerned as it is not with the concept of the equal validity of the claims of the good employer and the good worker, but with the principle that the economic privileges enjoyed by employers as a class can only be justified if they work to the greatest benefit of the least advantaged in society. Historically there can be little doubt that union power was exercised against employers in the interests of underprivileged, disadvantaged workers, and that the erosion of employer power advanced the cause of Rawlsian justice. But in the modern Western world many of the formerly exploited and underprivileged workers are now themselves economically privileged in relation, not only to the poor of the Third World, but to the poor in their own countries. Where union power is used to press the demands of the relatively privileged for wage increases well beyond rises in living costs and productivity, it is not the employers but the poor (the unemployed, the retired and the lowly paid) who will suffer from the resultant price increases. In resisting such demands employers might, irrespective of their personal motives, be seen as serving the ends of Rawlsian justice.

EMPLOYERS AND JUSTIFIED STRIKES

Both natural justice and Rawlsian justice enable one to distinguish between justified strikes and unjustified strikes, and to use the distinction to establish when workers are morally entitled to exercise the right to strike. But the concept of a justified strike is, I would argue, not without meaning and relevance for employers as well as for workers. To demonstrate this I will make use of Professor Hare's formulation of the universalization principle of morality, requiring moral judgements to be expressed in universal terms which the judge must be ready to have applied to himself were the roles in the moral judgement situation concerned reversed.[6] What I wish to argue, however, is, not that a moral judgement has no force if the judge is not willing to apply it to himself; but that, if a judge accepts the force of the judgement in a reverse role situation, he should apply it to himself.

Employer reversal judgements of justified strike action may be made either in employer or worker terms. The former might be expressed in the following moral rule:

Employer Rule 1

An employer ought to accept that his workers are justified in striking, if as an employer he accepts that workers would be justified in striking against another employer in a similar position.[7]

Rule 1 explicitly requires an employer to apply to himself the moral judgement he would make of another employer, and implicitly requires him to judge his own strike by putting himself in

6. See R. M. Hare, *Freedom and Reason*, Clarendon Press, Oxford, 1963.

7. A similar position is one where there are no differing features from those in the actual position relevant to the issue of whether or not strike action is justified.

85

the position of another employer faced with a similar strike. Judgements made without reference to the rule might still be morally valid in substance, if they would conform to the rule. What could not be established, however, is whether any particular employer judgement complied with, or conformed to, the rule, since the judgement is a purely subjective one. There is no way of determining whether an employer is lying if he asserts that he is morally convinced as an employer that no workers anywhere would ever be morally justified in striking in support of the demands being made by his striking workers; or whether he is simply expressing his judgement of his own strike in a universalized form covering all strikes, without having made any attempt to reach a valid non-partial judgement in the context of other employer strikes. Moreover, it has to be recognized that such a judgement requires an act of imagination, putting one's self in another's hypothetical situation, which some may find difficult.

These limitations are removed if, in point of fact, the employer has already made a judgement that another employer's workers were justified in taking strike action. A new and stricter moral rule may be formulated to meet this situation.

Employer Rule 2
An employer is morally obliged to accept that his workers are justified in striking, if he had in fact accepted that workers were justified in striking against another employer in a similar position in the past.

Rule 2 differs from Rule 1 in that the condition is no longer imaginary and hypothetical; it either has or it has not been met. If it has been met then the employer is strictly under an obligation to apply the judgement then reached to his own position. He cannot in conscience evade the issue or fail in the task of trying to face it. Moreover, if one knows that the judgement then reached was that strike action against another employer was justified, it is possible to expose the invalidity and immorality of any attempt to present a condemnation of his own strikers as not being contrary to the requirements of Rule 1.

With both moral rules there is a strong presumption of a corollary requiring the employer to meet the workers' strike demands, since an employer's conception of a justified strike is one which is in furtherance of demands which are just from the employer's standpoint as well as from the workers'. The presumptions may become requirements if the rules are differently formulated.

Employer Rule 1a
An employer ought to meet his workers' strike demands, if he accepts that another employer in a similar position ought to meet such demands.

Employer Rule 2a
An employer is morally obliged to meet his workers' strike demands, if he accepted that another employer in a similar position ought to have met such demands.

Before leaving employer judgements made from the employers' own standpoint, it is of interest to look at the moral situation created for an employer by a fellow employer's assertion of a moral obligation to meet his own workers' strike demands. This quite often occurred in the nineteenth century when individual masters refused to pay the 'going' rate. Indeed it was not unknown for masters paying the rate to coerce trade unions into taking strike action against 'rate-cutting' employers by themselves threatening to cut the rate paid.[8] What would be the moral force of rules expressed in one or other of the following terms?

Employer Rule 3a
An employer ought to meet his workers' strike demands if other employers in a similar position accept that such demands are justified and should be met.

Employer Rule 3b
An employer ought to meet his workers' strike demands if other

8. See *Minutes of Evidence Before Select Committee on Combinations of Workmen*, H.M.S.O., 1838, p. 31.

employers in a similar position have accepted such demands as justified and have met them.

It will be readily apparent that such moral injunctions are not grounded in the universality principle as traditionally formulated, appealing as they do to the individual not in terms of his own reason and conscience, but requiring him to take account of the general consensus of opinion of the group of which he is a member. If Rule 3b applies to a situation where the employer concerned has failed to give effect to a binding decision of an employers' association of which he is a member, then he has a quasi-legal obligation, not to his workers to meet *their* demands, but to *his* association, to apply *their* conditions. Conversely, an employer would be under an obligation to his association not to give effect to strike demands which he thought justified, if the granting of such demands were expressly contrary to employer association policy. The employer might, of course, sever such quasi-legal obligations by resigning from the association, leaving him, however, still subject to such moral force as there is in Rules 3a and 3b.

On examination it becomes apparent that the difference between these two rules is one not of substance but of the degree of reliance that can be placed on other employers' appraisals. With Rule 3b one can feel confident that these employers really mean what they say, since they have already applied to themselves the principle they are proclaiming. But can the fact that other persons in the same position as myself believe that all in that position ought to do X, create any obligation on me to do X? The answer must be 'No', except in the weak sense of an obligation to consider the *reasons* they give for doing X. Where employers in the same position as myself are unanimous in strongly urging that I ought to meet the demands of my own strikers, I ought to carefully reconsider my position to determine whether I am morally justified in refusing these demands. I am not under any obligation to carry out the moral injunctions of others, unless I believe them to be valid and applicable to me. What I am obliged to do is to ensure that the moral decision I adhere to is itself universalizable in accordance with Rule 2.

Employer justifications of strike action in worker terms involve a direct reversal of strike roles and may be expressed as follows:

Employer Rule 4
An employer ought to accept that his workers are justified in striking, if, as a worker in his own factory or in another factory in a similar situation, he would support the strike as a justified strike.[9]

This formulation broadly expresses a Rawlsian position, in that it requires the employer, as the advantaged, to make judgements from the standpoint of the rational interests of a worker, as the disadvantaged. Rule 4 is similar to Rule 1, in that it also requires the employer to place himself in an imaginary strike situation and to apply the judgement reached in that imagined situation to the actual strike situation he confronts. It is subject to even graver limitation than Rule 1, however, in that an employer might find it more difficult to imagine himself in the position of a worker than of another employer. He may thus be able to make a worker-based assessment of strike justification, or be liable to make an assessment which simply expresses the judgement he makes as an employer. There is one rather remote position in which these limitations would be removed; that is if he himself had, as a worker, actually supported strike action.

Employer Rule 5
An employer is morally obliged to accept that his workers are justified in striking, if in a similar past situation, he had, as a worker, supported strike action against his employer.

9. There is no moral difference in the position of an employer as an imagined worker in his own factory and as an imagined worker in another factory, but since the former requires the employer to see himself as a worker with a grievance against himself as employer, the latter's imagined position is likely to lend itself more readily to the making of a worker-based assessment of strike justification.

An employer in this situation, as in a Rule 2 position, would be strictly under an obligation to accept that his own workers were justified in striking; but there would be no presumption in this case, or in Rule 4 cases, of an inherent obligation to meet the workers' demands, since the justifications made are in worker not employer terms. A strike, reasonably held to be justified by workers, may not be seen as reasonably justified by employers, since they have different interests, concerns and vantage-points. Workers may strike for a 'fair wage' which employers may feel unable to pay in prevailing market conditions. Rawlsian justice, however, would seem to imply a strong *prima facie* obligation of employers to meet workers' just strike demands. What constitutes strike justification for workers will be considered in the next chapter.

Five

Workers and Strikers

Because the legal right to strike in Britain was recognized only negatively, through the removal of prohibitions and restrictions against established and extensive practices engaged in by workers in dispute with their employers, the law is only marginally relevant to the question of the rights of workers in strikes. Workers and their associations were left to their own devices, subject only to the limited provisions of the law relating to strikes, especially with regard to picketing, and to the general provisions of the criminal law. One particular consequence is that the law does not lay down and define the right of any worker not to go on strike. Since striking workers and their associations are concerned with defeating the employer, it is not surprising that they should have had little time for the notion of the rights of the non-striker. In particular the conception of an unqualified right of any worker not to join the strike is subversive of the principle of solidarity on which both strikes and trade unions alike depend. Worker solidarity is desirable in itself and as the necessary condition for securing the workers' objectives, whereas strikes and trade unions are but means to ends. Appeals to strike solidarity can be made on behalf of workers who are not unionized and to union members in spite of opposition from their own union.

Although the language of solidarity is the language of moral obligation, worker solidarity is not an open account on which any group of workers can draw. Solidarity has to be accorded; it cannot be imposed. Thus at some point or other in a developing strike situation those concerned, or potentially concerned, expect to have the opportunity to participate in the making of a collective decision. In terms of the principle of working-class solidarity that decision *ought* to be made with regard to the interests of the group of workers concerned (though problems may arise in deciding how extensive is the group to be considered), but there is nothing to prevent each of the participants from having prime or sole regard to his own selfish interests. It is for this reason that many staunch unionists are opposed to the use of secret strike ballots in place of strike meetings and open voting, since the former facilitates the expression of personal interest while the latter strongly encourages that of common interest. The adoption of either method, however, is accepted as producing a decision which is binding on all members of the group concerned, whether participant or absent, whether unionists or non-unionists, whether in the majority or the minority. This acceptance is in accordance with normal democratic theory and practice, subject to the proviso that all members of the group are eligible to participate. Thus, if a strike ballot were conducted amongst union members only, non-union members would not be bound by the decision as reached; although they might be expected to act, or be pressurized into action, in conformity with that decision.

More complex and difficult problems arise over the question of participation. Especially in partially organized firms with no strike record, some workers many not recognize the authority of a strike meeting and consequently not attend it for that reason, rather than from apathy. Such workers may then claim that they are in no way obligated by a strike meeting's decision, either because, in their view, it had no right to take any decision, or that any decisions it took were binding only on the participants. Such views are likely to be the more strongly expressed where the participants themselves are a minority of the total workforce in whose name the strike decision is made. Persuasive as such arguments may appear they require to be put into perspective. Given the nature of the way in which strike situations develop, the strike meeting is in most cases the *only* way in which collective decisions on strike action can be taken at local level. Objection to the use of strike meetings for reaching strike decisions expresses in many cases objections either to strikes *per se* or to their incidence. Those who believe in keeping the strike as a weapon ready to hand for workers on the shop floor will support the use of the strike meeting. Any other method, to a lesser or greater extent, reduces the opportunity for the exercise of initiative by members of the workforce and increases the power of union officials. The institutionalization of the strike would reduce its value and use as a means for direct spontaneous expression of feelings of grievance and discontent by those subject to the discipline of factory life. The strike meeting is perhaps the clearest expression to be found of industrial democracy at work.

A large proportion of strikes today exhibit the same quality of spontaneous demonstration that they did in the early period before trade unions were accepted by employers as entitled to exist, and before collective bargaining machinery was established. The first notice the foreman or shop steward may have of a strike on hand is when a group of men down tools and walk out of the shop. This is the simplest form which a strike can assume and as such it raises no problems of obligation – those who are aggrieved collectively exercise their right to strike without seeking to involve anyone else. Those who aren't aggrieved keep on working. The situation changes when those who walk out call on others to follow them, either on the grounds that the grievance is a common one or in the name of worker solidarity – 'one out, all out'. The appeal for assistance may well be couched in terms of duty, but as long as it is possible to reject such an appeal without fear of sanctions these other workers clearly retain the right individually to determine for themselves whether to respond to the duty call.

More commonly, however, a walk-out is a prelude to a strike meeting to determine whether or not to take strike action. Alternatively there may be a strike meeting without any walk-out. In either case the decision whether to strike is taken, not by a group of like-minded workers collectively agreed on a walk-out, nor by men individually in response to a personal appeal to 'join in', but by majority vote. The right to strike, as the right of each individual to decide whether to strike, is replaced by the very different and more limited right to participate in reaching a collective decision on strike action. Moreover from the nature of things that right will, for most participants, be limited to the right to vote by show of hands on a strike resolution. A strike meeting is not a forum for debate, but a gathering of workers to decide whether to respond to a strike call from some of their fellows. The underlying presumption behind a strike meeting is that there are grounds for strike action, otherwise there would be no meeting. Consequently those who attend are in a mood, and of a disposition, to be persuaded by those who initiated the meeting that strike action is both justified and necessary.

If a strike meeting is to provide what it is claimed to provide – a rational choice decision binding on all the workers concerned – the following conditions must be met:

1. All workers claimed as subject to the meeting's decision should:
(a) know that they are so claimed;
(b) know of the meeting;
(c) be entitled to attend;
(d) be entitled to ask questions;
(e) be entitled to vote on the strike resolution;
(f) not be subject to violence, intimidation or threats in the exercise of the right to vote.
2. The case for taking strike action should be clearly stated.
3. The strike resolution should spell out:
(a) the workers directly claimed as subject to the resolution;
(b) the strikers' demands.
4. If the strike resolution is carried, the meeting should determine:
(a) who is responsible for conducting the strike – if a strike committee, its composition should be agreed to;
(b) whether other workers should be called on to join the strike;
(c) when further strike meetings are to be convened.

Items 1(a)–1(f) may be regarded as the minimum rights which workers need to have accorded to them individually in a strike-meeting situation. If such rights are not accorded to any worker, then that worker cannot be held to be under any obligation to strike deriving from a decision of the strike meeting. While allowance has to be made in interpreting these conditions for the often confused and informal way in which such meetings are called and held, the conditions themselves can be, and commonly are, met in essence. It should be noted that, with the exception of 1(d) and 1(e), where the rights may be claimable from the person chairing the meeting, these rights are not rights against specific persons charged with the duty of abiding by these requirements. It is not a question of someone having the specific duty of ensuring that all workers on the shop floor know of the strike meeting, but rather that the existence of the opportunity to exercise the right of attendance and of voting freely is the prior minimum condition for any valid claim to be made against any worker or a number of workers being bound by the meeting's decision. It is worth stressing that failure to meet these minimum conditions would absolve the workers concerned from any obligation to comply with either a strike-meeting decision *to* strike or a decision *not to* strike, leaving the workers in the latter case with a right themselves to take strike action. The same considerations apply with regard to non-observance of the other conditions of obligation.

Condition 2 raises greater difficulties, especially when one recognizes both the complex nature and setting of most strike situations, and the different appraisals likely to be made of strike situations according to an individual's position, perspective and values. In Chapter 3 it was argued that, while strikes may serve purposes other than the expression of a grievance, only grievance strikes were accepted as legitimate within the practice of collective bargaining, and that these grievances, therefore, needed to be specified in terms capable of being settled in negotiation with the employers. But, while some strikes are the direct expression of grievances readily capable of formulation and decision at a strike meeting (e.g. a demand by dockers for extra money for handling a 'dirty' cargo), others are not. Continual frustration at the chopping and changing about on a new job may build up resentment to the point where men walk off the premises, before that frustration has found expression in a processable demand, e.g. for a higher rate for that job. In such circumstances the case for the strike has to be found and formulated *after* the walk-out. If the formulation of demands actually takes place through discussion at the strike meeting itself, this will mean that those attending will have had the unique opportunity to make their own case and formulate their own demands; instead of just to vote on what others have produced – which is what happens at most strike meetings. But if, as may happen, no clear case or set of demands emerge during the meeting, then the notion of obligation resulting from rational choice appears to break down.

No problem arises, of course, if the frustrated would-be strikers are unable to secure a majority for strike action. But what if they do secure majority backing, perhaps because they are themselves a majority of those present? Are all those present, as well as those absent, strictly bound to support strike action for unknown reasons and objectives? One answer would be, that no obligation *at all* can be derived from a decision of that sort. Indeed one might go further and argue that where no basis exists for making a valid or meaningful decision, what we have is not a decision but a happening, which cannot bind anyone. A loose analogy might be drawn with a crowd at a demonstration in which a majority takes up the cry of 'Get the Police'. Nobody in the crowd can be said to have any obligation to act out the intention expressed in the chant, neither those who make up the chanting majority, nor the silent minority. There is nothing of an obligation-creating nature in such a situation; though some participants in the crowd, as in the invalid strike meeting, may have established outside the crowd situation itself what are for them prior obligations which remain binding. The strike meeting is, of course, different from a crowd in that it is meant to create and is capable of creating obligations, but such obligations are not established by the mere display of a majority show of hands at a meeting of workers off the job.

The contrary view, to which many staunch trade unionists would doubtless adhere, is that, providing the workers at a meeting know they are voting on whether or not to strike, the absence of any clear statement of the case for and aims of the strike does not affect the validity and binding nature of the strike decision. On this view those dissatisfied with such a state of affairs can express that dissatisfaction by voting against strike action. But acceptance of this position involves conceding to a committed majority the moral right to use the strike meeting as a rubber stamp, not only to secure *carte blanche* advance approval for the strike action they are determined upon, but to bind all other workers to strike in support of their as yet unformulated purposes. The highly unsatisfactory nature of this situation can be in part removed if it is clearly laid down that strike claims and demands *when formulated* shall be put to a later strike meeting for endorsement or rejection. What it cannot remove, however, is the unsatisfactory nature of the proposition itself, with its demand that all are required to follow the majority, even though the latter are not only blind, but don't know where they want to go or why.

Since a strike involves both organizing the workers and conducting negotiations with the employer, it is apparent that some persons must be selected for these purposes. Where the authority for calling a strike derives from a strike meeting, then the meeting itself ought either to appoint the members of a strike committee or approve that function being carried out by those with established authority (e.g. the shop stewards), otherwise actions are likely to be taken to further the strike by persons who have no authority to act and are responsible to nobody for their actions. The scope of the authority of the strike committee or shop stewards may be defined by the strike meeting or, more usually, left open. Unless specifically determined on by the strike meeting to the contrary, the authority of the strike leaders is subject to the following implicit and inherent conditions:

1. A strike called by a strike meeting can only be terminated by a strike meeting.
2. A strike meeting should be called to consider any major development, e.g. a new management offer, which raises within the strike leadership the issue of whether to continue or end the strike.

The question of extending the strike is a crucial one in this context, since if the strike is extended it enlarges the population eligible to constitute the subsequent strike meetings. In particular it means that the decision to call off the strike no longer rests in the hands of those who called it. If the rights of the latter are to be protected it is necessary that they should themselves decide as a body whether to seek to extend their strike. This provides us with a third condition:

3. A strike meeting should be called to decide whether a strike should be extended.

Strikes may be extended in one of two ways – either by persuading a specially called meeting of workers in another section or shift at the factory to join the stoppage, or by persuading little gatherings of workers to do so. In the former case essentially the same considerations arise as those discussed above with relation to strike meetings except that:

1. The issue before the meeting of the second group of workers is not whether to *call* a strike, but whether to respond to a call from others to *join* a strike already called.
2. The call to join will always contain a strong element of moral appeal to worker solidarity, even if it is primarily couched in terms of common material interest.
3. What the meeting has to decide is whether (*a*) to associate itself with the demands formulated by the original strikers, or (*b*) to put forward demands of its own.

4. If it determines on 3(*b*), then either (i) agreement will be reached with the original group of strikers on a joint set of demands, or (ii) it will not.
5. In the event of 3(*a*) or 3(*b*)(i) it will be necessary to establish some joint body (e.g. joint strike committee) for running the joint strike, subject to the determination of the strike being left to the decision of a joint strike meeting, and to joint strike meetings being made aware of major new developments.[1]
6. In the event of 3(*b*)(ii) there will be two parallel strikes by different groups of workers each responsible for conducting and settling its own dispute. Each strike committee would, however, have a duty to consult the other, and to make their own strikers aware of major changes in the other strikers' position and views.

Rather different considerations arise where, as commonly happens, groups of workers at a particular shop or plant coming off, or going in to, work are directly approached by strikers and asked to join the strike. Here we appear to have a position where the individual worker has both the right and the opportunity to decide for himself whether to come out on strike. The strikers appeal for his own personal support, and he responds as he personally thinks fit. But it is important to note that, even where the appeal is made by a single striker to a single worker, it is made in the name of a group of strikers *a* to a member of another group of fellow workers *b* in terms of their common interests and loyalties. The appeal to strike in such circumstances is likely to take the form, not of a call to an individual to personally stop work, but of a call to him and others round about to shut down the whole shop or plant concerned – either by joining the strikers in persuading their mates not to go in to work, or by going in to persuade those

1. Where a strike spreads to different factories it will be impractical to hold joint meetings. Separate strike meetings and strike votes will bind only those workers separately covered, unless there is some agreement to the contrary (i.e. to abide by the overall majority secured on a common resolution put to all the separate meetings).

already at work to come out.[2] Consequently, while the individual worker in this position is generally accepted as having the initial right to decide for himself whether or not to join the strike, his personal determination not to strike is not accepted as final.

A new situation is created where those b group workers who exercised their right as individuals to choose whether to join a group's strike and chose to do so, (bi) are linked together with a group workers in what is now seen as a strike of a and b group workers in defence of a and b group common interests. Those b group workers who exercised their right as individuals not to join the a group strike, (bii) are perceived by the strikers, especially b strikers, as no longer having the right to persist in their choice. The adherence of bi workers is seen as transforming the nature of both the strike cause and the strike choice, establishing a moral obligation on bii workers to rally to the common cause in support of their fellow workers (bi). If that obligation is not recognized then the strikers, and especially bi strikers, are held entitled to exert collective pressure on bii workers to persuade them to change their minds. Where persons change their minds through fear or apprehension of the consequences of not doing so the pressure exerted is clearly coercive.

The non-strikers, for their part, are rarely united by any sense of common purpose and lack effective leadership; consequently they are left as isolated individuals to face the collective pressure of the strikers, often unaware even of the potential strength of their own position. That pressure may be successfully employed by a very distinct minority of the workforce who come out on

2. One of the initial strikers in the sheet-glass works at Pilkingtons in 1970 recalls how six of them set about trying to get the float-glass plant men out. 'We spoke to the shift going on the night shift and asked for their support. Some didn't want to know us, some said "Yes, we'll stop out now and stop the others going". But we told them not to do this, but to come in and let the afternoon shift off, not to start work and to try and persuade the others not to start – which they did, and did very effectively.' Tony Lane and Kenneth Roberts, *Strike at Pilkingtons*, Fontana, 1971, pp. 90–91.

strike is clearly brought out by the strike-sympathetic authors of *Strike at Pilkingtons*. Their own survey in the sixth week of the strike showed that only 20 per cent of strikers had initially welcomed the strike, although by the time of the survey 53 per cent thought the initial decision to strike had been justified. The authors found many strikers who complained of intimidation but they concluded that, with the exception of a few isolated instances of physical threats or violence, what such strikers encountered was moral pressure. Under that heading, however, they included the pressure exerted on workers coming off their own shift by the presence of thousands of strikers outside the gates, and the well-founded fear of sanctions being imposed against blacklegs by strikers after a return to work.[3]

There ought to be a clear distinction made between the use of social pressure to induce recalcitrant members of a group to abide by *that* group's collective strike decision to which they either contributed, or could have contributed, and the use of such pressure to persuade reluctant members of another group (*b*) to abide by your group's (*a*'s) strike decision. While it might be held that social pressure is justified to require members of group *a* to carry out *their* established obligations, it cannot be held justified with regard to group *b* members since no obligations have been established. Indeed it is readily apparent that no such obligations can be created simply through the individual decision of some group *b* members (*b*i) to support the group *a* cause. One might attempt to meet this fundamental objection in one of two ways – by establishing a subsequent binding obligation to strike for *b*ii members or a prior obligation to strike for all *b* group members. In the first case it might be argued that an obligation can be established for the coerced group *b* members after the event, if a majority at a meeting of members of both groups *a* and *b* votes to continue the stoppage – this was what happened in the Pilkington strike. This

3. ibid., Ch. 3, 'The Rank and File'.

plausible claim is vulnerable, however, as can be seen from an analysis of the composition of such a combined meeting (see Figure 1).

Figure 1   Composition of combined strike meeting of groups a and b.

Position of members entitled to attend / Obligations of members entitled to attend	Members who wanted to strike	Members who did not want to strike	Members who were undecided on strike action
Members under an obligation to strike (all a members)	a i	a ii	a iii
Members not under an obligation to strike (all b members)	b i	b ii	b iii

It has been argued that, if the group a strike decision vote reflects an uncoerced expression of the wishes of those present (i.e. ai $>$ $a$ii), then all members of group a have an obligation to strike. Similarly, if a separate strike meeting of group b members were held then all would be under an obligation to strike if bi $>$ $b$ii. But if a joint strike meeting of groups a and b is held, then a positive binding strike decision will be secured if ai $+$ bi $>$ $a$ii $+$ $b$ii. Such a result may be secured, in spite of the opposition of a majority of b group (bi $<$ $b$ii), if a is larger or more united in support of strike action than group b. The objection is not to the principle that a joint meeting of two groups can validly bind them all, even if a majority of one group is opposed to the decision reached; but to the assertion that such a decision is binding, even if the majority of the members of group b have already been coerced against their will into joining a's strike before the strike meeting. Indeed it is apparent that the original assertion implicitly requires some level of assent from members of both groups to the convocation of a joint meeting which shall bind them both. If most members of *b* refused to have anything to do with a meeting called by group *a* leaders and *b*i members, any strike decision reached would have little claim morally to commit all group *b* members.

The second point to note is that the joint strike meeting is a meeting of *a* and *b* group strikers to decide whether to continue *a*'s strike, not whether to call a strike. This is true for the members of both groups, but with the crucial difference that for group *b* members the point at issue is the continuance of a strike which as a group they never called and never decided to join, and which only *b*i members individually supported and voluntarily joined. Now that groups *a* and *b* are both on strike different considerations arise and it may well not seem politic for those who at a *b* group strike meeting would have voted against strike action (*b*ii) or abstained from voting (*b*iii), to vote now for an immediate return to work. Such considerations are likely to weigh even more strongly with *a*ii and *a*iii members who may indeed feel under, and will certainly be said by the pro-strike majority to *be* under, an obligation to continue to support strike action until the strike goals are secured. Thus it is likely that, especially in the early days of a widening dispute, the number of persons voting to continue the strike will be greater than the number of persons in group *a* who voted for the strike (*a*i) plus the number in group *b* who would have so voted (*b*i), given the opportunity.

What does this mean for the binding authority of the joint strike meeting? One might reasonably argue that group *b* members who attend to vote on the continuation of the strike are bound by the outcome of the vote, since their presence may be taken as acceptance of the right of the joint meeting so to decide and so to bind. Any *b*ii or *b*iii members who attend thereby put aside their right to be exempt from any claimed obligations to support a strike which they were required to join, as distinct from one which (like *b*i members) they chose to join. Some participants may wish to go further and assert that all would-be members are bound by the joint meeting decision to continue the stoppage. But while the participant group b members might be held, and probably hold themselves, by their attendance to have forgone their own right to be exempt from any claimed moral obligation to support a's strike, and to have bound themselves to accept the outcome of the joint meeting, it is not apparent that such members have any right to forgo the rights of, and accept obligations for, non-participant members of b group. Such a claim could only be validly made on the basis of an affirmative strike vote of a separate meeting open to group b members only.

Can the difficulties which arise in trying to establish under what conditions, and to what extent, group b members might *assume* an obligation to support group a members, be avoided by establishing a clear duty on the part of group b members to come to group a's aid? This second line of approach appears fruitful since, as we have seen, the principle of working-class solidarity underlies the values and practices of working-class organizations and experience. One may aver that the principle of working-class solidarity imposes on workers the duty to help each other in a strike situation, and go on to specify particular rights and duties, viz. a strict obligation not to do the work of anyone on strike and not to cross a picket line. But can one go further and specify that workers have a duty to respond positively to a strike call from their fellow striking workers? The answer must be 'No'. A negative duty of individual workers to refrain from frustrating or undermining a strike of fellow workers is very different from a positive duty of workers collectively to strike in support of their colleagues, even colleagues in another part of the same factory. Moreover it is apparent that no such strict positive duty is accepted by, or acceptable to, industrial workers. The authors of *The Social Organization of Strikes* analysed twenty-five strikes or near strikes in a vehicle manufacturing plant and in only seven cases was the strike justified by the strikers in terms of, and directed towards, the interests of workers as a collectivity. The remaining eighteen strikes were directed towards the interest of the workers as individuals.[4] It will be readily apparent that it is only in respect of strikes of the former category that claims can be made against outsiders for positive support – either on the grounds that their interests are directly involved, or that a vital principle is at stake. In terms of working-class principle and practice, workers on strike are expected to rely on themselves in any sectional dispute with management – they should only *appeal* for direct support if defeat threatens to very seriously weaken their own position (e.g. by dismissals), or to adversely affect their fellow workers. Even where the strike issue is seen by the strikers as one of general concern, this does not in itself entitle them to require others to join in, since those others are entitled to hold a different view. But if the principle of solidarity can only be validly invoked to require workers to support a strike in furtherance of common, as distinct from sectional, interests, there needs to be some agreed means whereby those whose support is being sought are given a say in determining whether the dispute should be accepted as one of general concern. Group *a* workers have no prior right to group *b* workers' support: still less are they entitled to put pressure on group *b* workers to join a strike about which they know virtually nothing, as happened in the Pilkington dispute.

A different set of problems arises if one considers strike action in the context, not of any group of workers, but, as usually happens, of workers who are members of a trade union. The first problem concerns the position of non-union members who will be ineligible to attend a union-called strike meeting. Such persons it would seem cannot be bound, as those eligible to attend may be bound, to abide by a strike meeting decision to down tools. As non-unionists they have the right to decide individually for themselves whether to *join in* the union members' strike – they cannot as outsiders actually *join* the strike. But this view is unlikely to be shared by the striking unionists themselves. The strike situation highlights the tensions between unionists and non-unionists by

4. Eric Batstone, Ian Boraston, Stephen Frenkel, *The Social Organization of Strikes*, Basil Blackwell, Oxford, 1978, pp. 59–62.

confronting the latter with the choice between complying with the will of the unionist strike-voting majority, or taking up a position of defiance. Where non-unionists are a small minority they will usually comply, through fear of social sanctions: where they are a substantial part or majority of the workforce they are much more likely to defy the union and risk the consequences.

As far as the union members are concerned no problems arise where union rules or union practice accept that in local disputes the union strike meeting is the body with authority both to call and end a strike. Shop stewards or union officials may recommend a particular course of action, but it is up to the strike meeting to take the decision which will bind the members. Indeed, since in local disputes the initiative invariably comes from below, it is virtually inconceivable that union officials in any union would attempt to impose a strike against the wishes, or without ascertaining the wishes, of the members through a strike meeting or strike ballot. Trade unions are not accepted by their members as having a right to impose their will on the members; especially where it is those members' interests which are at stake and those members who have to bear the burdens and risks involved in strike action.

Complications emerge in those unions where official approval is required for strike action to be taken, whether that approval be the approval of a specified official (e.g. the District Officer) or a specific body (e.g. the District or Executive Committee). It is necessary, however, to carefully distinguish between those cases where union approval is either by rule or conventional practice required only to make a strike 'official' (when strike pay will be made from union funds), and those cases where prior strike authorization is strictly required.[5] In the former cases it can

5. The gap between what the rules lay down and established practice is well illustrated in the Rules of the Yorkshire Area of the National Union of Mineworkers (1966), which state that 'no Branch or portion of a Branch shall be allowed to strike or leave off work, unless such course is sanctioned by two thirds of the members composing the Branch', to be ascertained by a Ballot Vote 'sanctioned by the Area Executive Committee of Area Council' (Rule 53a). It is doubtful whether anybody in the Union would expect such a procedure to be strictly followed in every minor dispute that arose.

reasonably be held that, provided members are aware that strike pay will not be forthcoming (and this is rarely at issue in the vast majority of short duration disputes), all members are bound by the decision of the strike meeting, where this involves no breach of the union-negotiated grievance procedure. The latter cases, on the other hand, contain the inherent prospect of a conflict of

Figure 2 Striker assessments of the authority of a union strike meeting to make a binding strike decision without the required approval of the union.

Possible conflict situations / Possible stances of strike meeting attenders	Decision to strike taken at strike meeting where attenders are:			
	(a) aware that union approval is required but will not be sought	(b) aware that union approval is required and will be sought	(c) unaware that union approval is required	(d) aware that union approval is required but will not be given
1. Strike meeting decision to strike binds unconditionally	Binding	Binding	Binding	Binding
2. Strike meeting decision to strike binding if trade union not officially opposed to strike action	Binding	Binding until and unless the union officially opposes strike	Binding	Not Binding
3. Strike meeting decision to strike binding only if trade union officially endorses strike	Not Binding	Binding until the union reaches a decision → then only binding if strike officially endorsed	Not Binding	Not Binding

authority between the strike meeting and the official union structure if the meeting determines on strike action without the required union approval. That conflict of authority, moreover, is not simply one between strikers and the union hierarchy, but one which finds expression within the ranks of the strikers themselves. This is illustrated in Figure 2 above.

Stance 3 is a strict one, difficult to hold, as it permits only officially endorsed strikes. Since it is such a strict view, its adherents may well refrain from strongly asserting their declared right not to abide by the strike meeting decision in (b) and (c) situations, especially if the union itself registers no outright condemnation of the strike. Stance 2 is vulnerable to moral criticism in situation (a), since it involves support for a policy of not carrying out one's responsibility to seek union approval in order to avoid having to apply one's own principles. The real crunch, however, comes in situation (d), or in (b), if the union response is outright opposition. In the case of (d) the following lines of argument might be employed by those who wish to establish their right not to abide by the strike meeting decision to take strike action:

1. As it was known that union approval was required, and would not be given, no strike meeting should have been held, since such a meeting had no authority to decide whether or not to take strike action.
2. Any meeting held had no right to take any decision to strike.
3. The strike meeting decision to strike was not binding and members had a right to ignore it.
4. Workers who remained at work could not be held to be strike-breakers.

The weakness of this strictly deductive line of reasoning is its failure to recognize that trade unions exist, not to apply rules, but to carry out their members' wishes and to provide a vehicle for the exercise of their rights, including the right to strike. Union rules are subordinate to union purposes. A demand for the strict application by ordinary union members of a rule requiring prior union authorization of each and every strike act, requires those suffering from an intense and urgent grievance to give way to the decisions of remote officials who may be, or be seen to be, ignorant of the true state of affairs, or inept in their handling of local issues. Union rules do not have for union members the moral status of the Ten Commandments, or the procedural status of Erskine May's *Parliamentary Practice*. They may need to be modified or even ignored where their strict application would undermine more fundamental principles or frustrate crucial purposes. Nevertheless, even on this view, non-compliance with union rules would require specific justification – in this case the substantiation of adequate and relevant grounds for overriding the union's right of strike veto.

It is doubtful, however, whether union officials themselves would develop the kind of strict constitutionalist argument outlined above; not only because it would be highly unpopular with many members, but because union members and officials at all levels recognize that strike meetings *are* legitimate sources of authority. Consequently, while a strike decision might be held to require union endorsement if it is to be binding in terms of the union's rules, even without such endorsement it is not held to be without authority over those members directly concerned. That is to say, union officials may well hold that, while a strike meeting decision is not binding on them, it is binding on those who participated. Where union officials address meetings of strikers they are more likely to seek to persuade members to accept the union's reasons for not supporting strike action than to demand members' compliance with the union's decision made in accordance with the rules. Union officials may well not challenge the authority of the meeting to reach a decision, not only because such a challenge might well be counter-productive, but because concepts of grass-roots democracy are part of the very stuff of union thinking. Members may be held to be wrong in going against the rules and voting for strike action, but it does not follow that those who voted against a strike will be regarded as having no obligation to comply with the majority strike decision. On the contrary, in the absence of express union authorization not to strike such members will be held in trade union thinking to be bound by the strike decision. A union would be unlikely to give such authorization not to strike, since it would create a major confrontation situation with the local membership and divert attention away from the central issue of the flouting of union authority. That issue is not whether *some* members are entitled to stay at work, but whether *any* members are entitled not to. If the gage is thrown down, local members have to decide whether to accept the authority of the strike meeting or that of the union and its rules.

Frequent and bitter conflicts between union officials and union strikers can be avoided only if unions refrain from seeking to deny the grass-roots authority of strike committees. But although this works reasonably well in situations where a dispute is likely to be of short duration and of limited outside impact, problems arise where the 'official' support of the union is sought in a protracted dispute, or is required in view of a strike's serious repercussion on other workers in the same or other unions. If the conduct of the dispute is handed over to the union's officials it might appear that such officials have been accorded full authority to settle the dispute as they think fit. But from the strikers' position, handing over the dispute does not mean recognition that officials have the right to reach binding agreements over the heads of the strikers. The union official is quite properly seen as the union member's agent, not his master, and striking members have a minimum right to expect that their representatives will be consulted in the course of negotiations on their claim. Whether the strikers claim a right to have any settlement reached made subject to the endorsement of a meeting of strikers will turn, not simply on what the rule book says, or on what was agreed with the officials concerned, but on the importance of the issue and the expectations aroused. Where the union is strong and active the need to conclude an agreement that will hold on the shop floor will push the officials into doing their damnedest to negotiate a settlement acceptable to their striking members. Where, on the other hand, the union is relatively weak, and the employers resistant, the officials may find themselves compelled to settle on terms which fail to meet the strikers' minimum expectations. It is precisely in such situations that the strongest case exists for making union-concluded agreements subject to the approval of the strikers concerned, even though this involves the possibility that they reject the best terms available. What cannot be condoned is any settlement which does not provide for the re-engagement of strikers. A union has the responsibility of exerting its power to the full to secure the re-engagement of strikers involved in an officially approved strike.

The problem is more straightforward where a trade union, in accordance with its rules, officially calls out its members on strike, as in a national stoppage. Such members then have a duty to obey the strike call and the union can exercise its right to impose sanctions in accordance with the rules against those members who refuse to comply. Further, one cannot accept that members have a moral right to resign from membership in order to evade obligations and sanctions freely accepted as a condition of such membership – sanctions may reasonably be applied against such 'fair-weather' members. Just as a union has the right to call its members out on strike, it has the right to conclude the stoppage, and the members a duty to comply accordingly. Members in local branches are not entitled to continue on strike simply because they are not satisfied with the terms of a national settlement reached, since the possibility of this outcome is inherent in the nature of national negotiating.

Unions formulate major wage claims in the knowledge that the process of negotiating requires that *both* parties must satisfy their respective members that some concessions have been secured from the other side. Unions thus pitch their claims above, and employers their offers below, what they are prepared to settle for. The union side, unlike the employer side, finds it necessary, however, to present the full claim to its members as the minimum to which they are entitled. Consequently, even a negotiated settlement which represents in full what the union negotiators were originally aiming at in formulating the claim, may appear to many members as an unwarranted back-down from their minimum entitlement. For this reason there is much to be said for unions making the calling-on and calling-off of national stoppages subject to ballots of the membership. The miners' method of holding such ballots at the pit head after each shift is particularly attractive, since it gives every N.U.M. member the right to vote, but under conditions which encourage voting by reference to collective rather than personal interests. Voting in this way promotes that sense of fraternity and community which underlies all that is best in trade unionism, whereas postal voting promotes the quite different values of individual self-interest.

WORKERS AND JUSTIFIED STRIKES

Whereas hiring and firing, applying for and leaving a job, are acts of individual determination, a strike decision is a collective determination to act, in the strict sense of being something more than the summation of individual determinations made in terms of rational self-interest. The essence of a strike situation is that those concerned see themselves as 'members one of another' with overriding common interests requiring resolute common action in the face of a common danger. The question those involved are expected to ask themselves is not, 'Is it right for me, is it in my interest to go on strike?', but 'Is it right for us, is it in our interests?' to do so. That is not to say that everyone will approach a strike decision in these terms, but simply to assert that the nature of a strike situation strongly inclines the participants to adopt such an attitude. This simple fact of strike-life creates major problems when one seeks to apply to workers the universalization principle for reversal judgements of strike justification used in the previous chapter in relation to employers.

For employers the question at issue in reversal judgements is whether a strike is justified: for workers it is whether a strike is unjustified. Worker reversal judgements in a strike situation may be made either in other-worker or in employer terms. The former may be expressed in the following moral rule:

Worker Rule 1
An individual worker in a strike situation ought to accept that the workers are not justified in striking against their employer, if, as a worker, he accepts that the workers would not be justified in striking against another employer in a similar position. A similar position is defined as one where there are no differing features from those in the current strike situation relevant to the question of whether or not strike action is justified.

A rule requiring a worker to judge a strike in his own factory by the standards he would apply to an outside strike is one which it may be difficult for the individual worker to give effect to, and impossible for anyone else to appraise, unless the worker concerned has in fact made such an outside-strike assessment, in which case we may postulate:

Worker Rule 1a
An individual worker in a strike situation is morally obliged to accept that the workers are not justified in striking against their employer if he had in fact, as a worker, accepted that workers were not justified in striking against an employer in a similar position in the past.

Worker Rule 1a imposes a strict and specific obligation on worker *a* where the factual condition has been positively met in his case; an obligation which may be properly laid at his door by any *x* who is aware of the fact. It is necessary, however, to make clear precisely what is *a*'s obligation. The rule itself is a rule of moral consistency which must be followed if a worker is to make a valid strike judgement. It in no way rules out differing judgements by different individuals. Thus worker *b* at the same factory who had not accepted that workers were not justified in striking in the earlier strike, or worker *c* who had no knowledge of that strike, must be accepted as equally entitled with *a* to make their own judgements as to whether a strike now would be justified. Consequently *a* is not required to assert, and *x* is not entitled to

113

assert, that collectively the workers are, as a matter of objective moral fact, not justified in striking. Rule 1a, therefore, needs to be expressed in a different and more restricted form.

Worker Rule 1b
An individual worker is morally obliged to accept that he is not entitled to claim that the workers are justified in striking against their employer, if he had in fact, as a worker, accepted that workers were not justified in striking against an employer in a similar position in the past.

May it be argued from the new form of the Rule that worker *a* has another and more specific obligation – not himself to go on strike? The answer is a qualified 'Yes'. An unjustified action for me is an action I am not morally entitled to take, and therefore, one I am under a moral obligation not to take, in the absence of other overriding moral considerations. This means that *a* is under a strict obligation not to strike in those conditions where he has an unquestioned right to determine for himself whether or not to strike. But a strike situation is rarely one where such an unquestioned right of individual determination can be claimed, since in most cases some body, such as a union or strike meeting, may claim authority to decide not whether the workers have a *right* to strike, but whether they have a *duty* to do so. In the exceptional circumstances where no binding strike decision has been made, e.g. where men walking off the job appeal to their colleagues, or where men on strike appeal to other workers as individuals to join them, we may formulate a new moral rule.

Worker Rule 2
An individual worker is morally obliged not to respond to a personal appeal from striking workers to take strike action if he had in fact, as a worker, accepted that workers were not justified in striking against their employer in a similar position in the past.

It is important to note that while Worker Rule 2 is the moral equivalent of Employer Rule 2 the practical implication of the two Rules is very different. In the second case there is a strong presumption that the individual employer should meet his workers' demands (a presumption which becomes a requirement in Employer Rule 2a), i.e. by terminating the strike to the workers' advantage: in the first only a requirement that individual workers in the same position as *a* should not respond to a strike call. Only in the unlikely event of there being a large number of workers in the same moral position as *a* would their giving effect to Worker Rule 2 be likely to affect the course of the strike. An individual employer who recognizes a strike as justified can easily bring it to an end: an individual worker who sees it as unjustified, cannot.

A strict worker appraisal of strike justification would be one made in employer terms as follows:

Worker Rule 3
An individual worker ought to accept that the workers are not justified in striking against their employer if, as the employer in his own factory or another factory, he would not accept the strike as justified.

It is revealing that this reversal proposition appears much more questionable than its Employer rule 4 equivalent (p. 89 above). For some this may reflect the defensive role which employers now play in industrial relations, where power and initiative now lie with the workers and their organizations: for others the moral superiority of the workers' case deriving from their disadvantaged social and economic position. Economic individualism and moral realism would tend towards the former stance; Marxism and Rawlsianism to the latter, leaving natural justice as the only direct supporter of the employer reversal rule. In practice, it is unlikely that workers would see or consider strike justification in this way, and those who did so, might be expected to find it more difficult to envisage themselves in an employer position than employers would in a worker position. The chances of any worker having actually been an employer in a similar strike position and therefore morally obliged to accept the judgement then made as employer, are very remote. Moreover, since the obligation imposed would not carry a presumption (as Employer Rule 5 does) of a duty to do what the other side wanted (concede strike demands or not join the strike), the practical implications of any rule so formulated would be negligible.

The limitations of the rules considered above stem from the fact that, while individual workers may join strikes as individuals, strikes are normally called, and often joined, through the decisions of trade unions or strike meetings. It has been argued above that, provided a strike is called officially by a union in accordance with its rules, or by a properly called and conducted strike meeting, those covered by the union or meeting are obliged to abide by the decisions so reached. In particular such decisions will override obligations created by the individual Worker Rules already outlined.

If we consider strike justification from the perspective of strike meetings it is apparent that we cannot use employer-role reversal terms, since it makes no sense to ask a strike meeting to put itself or think itself into the employer's position. A strike meeting is a collection of individual workers each of whom has the responsibility of deciding for himself on the justification for strike action, but where each individual participant is bound, not by his own moral judgement, but by the collective decision. For these same reasons it is impossible to require a strike meeting to apply to its own strike the standards it would apply to a hypothetically 'similar' strike. The first possible Strike Meeting Moral Rule one might put forward would be:

Strike Meeting Rule 1
A strike meeting ought to accept that it is not justified in calling a strike if a strike meeting of the same group of workers in the past decided that it or another group of workers in a similar position was not justified in taking strike action.

But it is difficult to see how a strike meeting can itself be bound by the prior decision of another strike meeting, even one of workers in the same group. Each strike meeting is a sovereign body, bound by no precedents and composed of different individuals. The most that one might claim is that it has a duty to take cognizance of the decisions reached at the earlier meeting.

Strike Meeting Rule 1a
(i) *A strike meeting of a group of workers who, at a previous strike meeting, had decided that it or another group of workers in a similar position was not justified in striking, ought not to accept that it would be justified in striking now unless reasons are adduced for not applying that decision in this case.*

(ii) *Each worker at the strike meeting who voted with the majority at the previous meeting has an obligation to vote against strike action if he does not find relevant and adequate the reasons adduced for striking now in similar conditions.*

We must now consider the problem from the standpoint of the trade union itself as a decision-making body. Thus we may express the basic Trade Union Moral Rule and its corollary in the following terms:

Trade Union Rule 1
A union ought to accept that it is not justified in taking strike action if it would not accept that another union in a similar position would be justified in taking strike action.

Trade Union Rule 1a
A union is morally obliged to accept that it is not justified in taking strike action if it had in fact accepted that another trade union in a similar position was not justified in taking strike action.

As with Employer Rules 1 and 1a (pp. 85 and 87 above), if Rule 1 applies then a valid moral judgement on strike action can be made only if it does not conflict with the Rule: while in a 1a situation there is a specific obligation on the part of the union concerned not to take strike action. There is, of course, in all these situations always the possibility that those concerned will argue that the situation is not 'similar', i.e. that there are differing factors which materially concern the issue of justification, factors which if they had been present in the other strike situation would have resulted in a different assessment. This problem cannot be resolved, but one can insist that if there is *prima facie* evidence to suggest that the cases are 'similar' then the onus is on the union concerned to demonstrate that there are significantly different factors which tip the scale from non-justified to justified strike action. One factor which might tip the balance is the experience of the consequences flowing from the decision in the earlier strike situation, e.g. a decision not to strike which led to a serious worsening of conditions.

But Trade Union Moral Rules may be expressed not only from the standpoint of the union judging but of the union judged. Thus we have two candidate rules:

Trade Union Rule 2
A union ought to accept that it is not justified in striking if other unions in a similar position accept that it is not justified in striking.

or

Trade Union Rule 2a
A union ought not to take strike action if other unions in a similar position have accepted that they were not justified in striking.

Much the same arguments apply here as with Employer Rules 3a and 3b discussed above (pp. 87–8). There can be no strict obligation on a union to abide by other unions' judgements; only an obligation to consider the reasons which led the other unions to come to contrary judgements. This obligation will be particularly strict where the consequences of taking a contrary view in favour of strike action have serious adverse effects on the members of the other unions concerned. Since unions rest on and affirm the principle of working-class solidarity this position may be given moral rule status.

Trade Union Rule 3
A union has an obligation to consider and answer objections against that union taking strike action raised by other unions who

claim that the strike position is similar to one in which they held
strike action to be unjustified.

One final situation may be considered, where a trade union may
be held to be morally bound by the strike decision of some other
body to which it belongs, e.g. the Trades Union Congress (T.U.C.).
The T.U.C. itself has no power to bind its members to take or
refrain from strike action, limiting itself to advice and exhortation. The only union body which might be thought of as having
binding strike powers is a Conference of Union Executives, and it
was such a Conference which in 1926 authorized the T.U.C. to
take general strike action. Since, however, that authorization was
given by a roll-call of trade unions it is not apparent that those
few unions which did not pledge support were 'constitutionally'
bound by the consenting majority. In the event the non-striking
unions, of which the National Sailors and Firemen's Union was the
most important, though morally condemned were not expelled
from the T.U.C.

The problem of what constitutes a justified strike for workers
has been analysed so far by reference to the rules of moral validity
which may be adduced from the universalization principle. But
the only cases in which the rules adduced prohibit some form of
positive action in relation to a strike are those situations where an
individual (Worker Rule 2), a strike meeting (Strike Meeting Rule
1aii), or a trade union (Trade Union Rule 1a) has, in point of fact,
made a previous determination that strike action in a 'similar'
position was not justified. Such situations are likely to be both
rare in themselves and difficult to substantiate, especially with
regard to establishing the essential 'similarity' of the strike situation. The question therefore arises whether it is possible to lay
down any substantive principles or guidelines as to what constitutes a justified strike, as distinct from rules of moral validity
relating to judgements of strikes as justified. In this connection it
is highly significant that a 1973 official survey showed the great
majority of workers and union activists, while holding strong
views on some strike issues, did not regard themselves as justified

in striking in any situation where they thought that it would be to their advantage to do so; a position which would accord with both the Marxist and moral realist standpoints.

Figure 3 Justification of strike or other industrial action in breach of procedure.[6]

Workers justified if	Employers' views	Shop stewards' views	Union officers' views
Management has broken an agreement	67%	76%	65%
Management appears to be resorting to unreasonable delay in dealing with grievances	60%	74%	72%
There is no other way of preventing the unfair discharge of a workmate	66%	80%	75%
In any situation where they think by acting in this way they can get what they want	22%	24%	13%

A strong case can be mounted in support of the majority claims that workers are *prima facie* justified in taking strike action where management has broken an agreement, resorted to unreasonable delays in handling grievances, or sacked a workmate unfairly. If workers have reasonable grounds for believing that they do in fact face one or other of these situations, then they are justified in taking strike action. The only caveat one might enter is that management should be afforded the opportunity to provide immediate redress or an explanation before strike action is taken. It is, of course, only to be expected that in many cases workers and management will have opposing views on whether agreements have been broken, unreasonable delays resorted to, or workers sacked

6. *Workshop Industrial Relations 1973: An enquiry carried out on behalf of the Department of Employment by Stanley Parker*, Tables 110, 111, A71, H.M.S.O., 1975.

unfairly;[7] but it is the reasonably held worker convictions on this score, not management convictions, which provide grounds for a justified exercise by workers of their right to strike. But what constitutes a reasonably held conviction? Must anything asserted as reasonable be accepted if there is no clear evidence to the contrary?

It is readily apparent that no definitive answer can be given to these questions, but it is possible to indicate lines and principles which, if not followed, throw grave doubts on the reasonableness of the stated conviction. The first line is to use the universalization reversal rules of strike justification outlined above. Thus one could underline that it is not a reasonable conviction to hold that one's own strike is a justified strike and another 'similar' strike not justified, unless one can show *relevant and adequate* grounds which 'tip the balance' in the former case; where *relevant* and *adequate* grounds would be grounds which workers in the latter case could be expected to accept as *relevant* and *adequate*. If we had an actual situation where such a 'similar' strike of *b* group workers had been judged unjustified by *a* group workers who now proposed strike action, then the refusal of *b* group workers to accept that there were *adequate* and *relevant* grounds distinguishing the two positions would cast grave doubts on any contrary assertion by *a* group workers. It would not necessarily invalidate such an assertion, however, since it is possible for two persons or groups of persons conscientiously to make different rational judgements on the essential 'similarity' of two strike situations. Moreover, it is not only *a* group workers who wish to claim the right to strike in what they assert to be a different situation, who may, consciously or unconsciously, put forward a biased assessment: *b* group workers may claim that *a* group's position is no different from theirs, precisely because *a* group did not then support *b*'s strike. Clearly *b* group has an obligation conscientiously to consider on its merits *a* group's case for *relevant*

7. ibid. Table A68 shows that 79 per cent of shop stewards, but only 26 per cent of foremen stated that disputes procedure within the workshop had been exhausted before their most recent strike took place.

and *adequate* grounds of difference between the two strike situations.

A quite different line of approach directs attention at the reasons given for taking strike action. It is illuminating, and in my view encouraging, that the strongest support was shown in the 1973 Workshop inquiry for strike action to prevent the 'discharge of a workmate unfairly', since what is here being asserted is not a right of workers to take justified strike action in support of their own interests, but a right to strike in support of another's interests; where that 'another' is a fellow worker to whom one is bound by ties of mutual obligation. Such mutual obligation may, indeed, be seen as imposing on 'workmates' a *duty* to strike, a duty which can be expressed in reciprocal terms.

Workmate Rule 1
A worker has a duty to support strike action on behalf of a fellow worker if he would hold his fellow workers to be under an obligation to take strike action on his behalf if he were in a similar position.

This rule gives expression to the underlying principle of trade unionism – worker solidarity – a conception which requires as a corollary the duty of ordinary members to take action in support of union activists threatened with, or made subject to, disciplinary action by the management because of union activities.

Workmate Rule 1a
A worker has a duty to support strike action on behalf of a union official or shop steward threatened with dismissal or other serious disciplinary action, if he would hold his fellow workers to be under an obligation to take strike action on his behalf if he were in a similar position.

In both cases the conditional obligation arising out of the 'similar' position would need to take account of the responsibility of the person concerned for getting himself into that position.

Thus if a worker is sacked for persistent bad timekeeping my assessment would be made, not on the basis of what I would hope my fellows would do for me *as* a bad timekeeper, but on whether I believe I would be entitled to call on others to strike on my behalf *if* I were to become a persistent bad timekeeper.

Finally we may look at the justification for taking strike action in terms of whether such action is undertaken or contemplated only as a *last resort*, i.e. when all other means reasonably available for settling the grievance concerned have been tried and failed. It will be immediately apparent that the *last resort* rule, as with all other rules discussed, applies only to strikes conceived as a rational choice response to an expressed grievance (see pp. 61–2). While the *last resort* rule finds no support from Marxists and has no standing for moral realists it is strongly favoured in conceptions of natural justice. More immediately to the point, it has a long and respectable union pedigree. Dedicated unionists who cannot be suspected of unwillingness firmly to prosecute justified strike causes have spoken up strongly on its behalf. Thus Tom Mann and Ben Tillett, the two great militant leaders of the famous dock strike of 1889, wrote at the time 'respecting strikes, we are fully aware that they should be "avoided wherever possible, and only entered into after other efforts at settlement have failed" . . . To cite what the dock labourers have done . . . A Committee of Arbitration [of the union] has been elected to whom all disputes must be referred, and no strike pay is allowed to members who take it upon themselves to strike, thus ensuring opportunities for discussion which generally result in a settlement'.[8]

While it is not possible, except in relation to the facts of a particular case, to say whether a *last resort* situation has been reached; and while there is considerable room for disagreement as to what constitutes a *last* resort, a high proportion of unofficial stoppages are clearly not *last resort*, since the majority of such stoppages are taken without reference to the established collective

8. Tom Mann and Ben Tillett, *The 'New' Unionism*, pamphlet, 1890.

bargaining or dispute procedures. The formulation of a *last resort* strike rule should take proper account of this fact.

Last Resort Strike Rule

1. *The only strikes which workers or unions are justified in calling are 'last resort' strikes.*
2. *A 'last resort' strike is one called where either:*
(a) *the established disputes procedure has been tried and failed* or
(b) *where compelling grounds can be adduced to override the requirement to exhaust the disputes procedure before striking.*

Prima facie grounds for asserting that compelling overriding grounds have been adduced might be claimed in any of the following circumstances:

1. Management has broken an agreement to the detriment of the workers concerned.
2. Management has resorted to unreasonable delays in operating the collective bargaining or disputes procedures.
3. Only immediate strike action can prevent:
(a) a gross violation of rights which would be difficult to remedy if action is delayed (e.g. dismissal of shop steward);[9]
(b) threat of serious injury (e.g. unsafe machinery), or serious discomfort (e.g. lack of adequate heating or ventilation);
(c) unilateral management introduction of major changes which have significant adverse consequences for the workers concerned (e.g. large-scale redundancies).

The universalization rules outlined earlier may be helpful in some cases for substantiating whether the *prima facie* grounds adduced for *broken* agreements, *unreasonable* delays, *violation* of rights, *threat of serious* injury or discomfort, *unilateral imposition* of *significant adverse* changes, can be morally substantiated in the

9. A shop steward might well be eligible for legal compensation for wrongful dismissal, but that would not constitute a remedy for the workers being deprived of his leadership and for the weakening of union organization within the workshop.

face of judgements which can be made in 'similar' positions. Regard must also be paid to the nature of the industrial climate in the factory if a meaningful assessment is to be made of the reasonableness of any union claim that urgent necessity overrides the need to exhaust the disputes procedure. Unconstitutional necessity is the child of bad industrial relations.

In the chapter which follows the issue of strike justification is examined in the wider context of the rights of the public and the duties of the State.

Six

Public Rights and Government Duties

The right to strike is distinctive in that its exercise commonly results in considerable inconvenience for, or injury to, the interests of persons not party to the dispute concerned. These undesired and undesirable consequences arise out of the nature of the employment relationship itself and do not result only from the actions of workers. Thus the exercise of the traditional employer right to fire at will frequently causes serious hardship not only to the workers dismissed but to outsiders. The closure of a major factory, or a major cutback in its labour force, can mean that many other workers in dependent or associated firms are also made redundant. In some cases this may lead to a general run-down of a whole area, a falling-off in the level of rate-funded services, and a general deterioration in the quality of life of the inhabitants. Public authorities, too, are the authors of measures which result in a reduced level of services – closing local schools or hospitals, cutting back or abolishing rail services – measures adopted at the time in the name of efficiency and public interest. But just as we cannot avoid some level of inconvenience and suffering resulting from public bodies carrying out their public duties, or private bodies exercising their private rights, so one cannot expect to avoid the publicly more obvious, but not necessarily socially more serious, ill effects of workers operating their right to strike. Indeed one may go further and say that, insofar as one accepts the right to strike as a fundamental right which men should have, some level of public inconvenience must be accepted, since that is the price of having fundamental rights. Alternatively, one may argue that, since inconvenience is an inherent rather than an incidental consequence of the right to strike, it is questionable whether it should be accepted as a fundamental right at all – an issue which will be taken up in the final chapter. If one accepts the principle that there ought to be a guaranteed right to strike, at least in the minimum sense of there being no general legal prohibition against workers taking strike action, one may then consider the respects in which the exercise of that right may conflict with other fundamental rights of citizens – which it is the responsibility of Governments to secure and protect. The crucial areas of concern to citizens may be classified as follows:

1. Protection of the realm from the threat of external aggression.
2. Maintenance of the rule of law.
3. Protection of the right to work.
4. Provision of essential supplies and services.
5. Maintenance of freedom of expression.

It has to be recognized that a discussion in these terms involves acceptance of the conception of persons as members of a community with certain shared interests and values. It is thus incompatible with an approach which sees the State as essentially an instrument of class rule and the rights of man in bourgeois society as the rights 'of egoistic man . . . an individual separated from the community, withdrawn into himself, wholly occupied with his private interest and acting in accordance with his private caprice' (Marx)[1], whose interests and needs can be realized only as a social being in a socialist society.

1. Protection of the realm

The right of the citizen to be protected and the duty of the Government to protect the realm against its foes are universally upheld. In a major war unions normally agree to the withdrawal of the right to strike for the duration of hostilities, either in vital war industries (Britain after 1915), or in all industries (Britain after 1940). But, in spite of the fact that in both World Wars only an insignificant minority of workers adopted a position of oppo-

1. Karl Marx, 'On the Jewish Question', 1843, in Robert C. Tucker, *The Marx-Engels Reader*, second edition, W. W. Norton, New York, 1978, p. 43.

sition to the war, strikes continued to take place. Indeed the number of days lost in strikes during the Second World War was roughly the same as the number lost in the same period before the war, and more than in the period immediately following; while the figure for 1944 (the year of the Allied landings in France) was higher than for any year since 1932 and until 1955, in spite of a strenuous campaign against strikes waged by the trade unions on the one hand and the Communist party on the other.[2] Two thirds of the days lost through strikes in 1944 resulted from two miners' disputes which caused widespread strikes in the pits. But while the loss of coal through disputes was three times as high in 1944 as it had been in 1938, this was much less serious than the doubling of the rates of absenteeism, and more especially the 10 per cent fall in the output per man shift at the coalface. The authors of *British War Economy* conclude that 'the causes of this decline in output per man shift at the face were partly physical – an ageing labour force was feeling the strain of working $5\frac{1}{2}$ shifts or more a week – and partly due to a smouldering discontent over wages, the working of the Essential Work Order in relation to absenteeism and a whole range of problems of pit upkeep and organization'. On the other hand, during the years of Hitler's triumphs in 1940 and 1941 coal output per man shift was maintained at a pre-war level, while the number of shifts was $6\frac{1}{2}$ per cent higher, and the tonnage lost through disputes was less than half the pre-war figure.[3] This suggests that, while it may be necessary officially to ban strikes in wartime, it is unrealistic, and indeed un-

2. Strikes were banned in Britain from 1940 to 1951. Between 1945 and 1950 there were some 10,000 illegal stoppages involving nearly three million workers, but not a single striker was prosecuted until the autumn of 1950. The imprisonment then of ten leaders of a strike of 1,700 gas maintenance workers led to an outcry from the trade unions and to the revocation of the Order prohibiting strikes and lock-outs. See Eric Wigham, *Strikes and the Government 1893–1974*, Macmillan Press, 1976, Ch. 6.

3. W. K. Hancock and M. M. Gowing, *British War Economy* (History of the Second World War: United Kingdom Civil Series, edited by Sir Keith Hancock), H.M.S.O. and Longmans, Green & Co., 1949, Ch. 16, 'Coal and Transport', p. 471.

reasonable, to expect workers to refrain from strikes no matter what their grievances. Legal proscription may deter some groups of workers from taking strike action, but it is unlikely to have much effect on groups, like the miners, with strong traditions of industrial militancy and contempt for laws restricting union activities. The miners relied on class solidarity to protect them from prosecution, as it did when the authorities unwisely undertook proceedings at the Betteshanger Colliery in 1941. There is much to be said for the misgivings expressed by the then Lord Advocate for Scotland, 'at finding in the code of emergency legislation a new criminal offence of which the criminal authorities seldom dare take cognizance and which, in the majority of cases, the public may therefore safely ignore'.

The Ministry of Labour's own policy was to treat most unofficial stoppages as brief spontaneous outbursts which 'could be regarded as a safety valve and a reaction to war-time conditions accentuated by strain and fatigue. The question of prosecution should not arise unless the Ministry was satisfied that a stoppage was associated with subversive activities, or malicious intent by individuals taking part, or wilful and obstinate refusal to accept the discipline of the law and their own union'. The alternative to such a gentle application of the law was 'a far more drastic limitation of freedom in industry than is represented in this order, and this would probably produce an industrial situation which might well make prosecution of the war impossible'.[4] This question has been dealt with at some length because it well illustrates the dangers and difficulties of making rash judgements and interventions when confronted with strike problems. If it is open to serious doubt whether strikes should be forbidden in war time, and, if forbidden, whether the prohibitions should be implemented except in rare instances, it is apparent that one should be even more hesitant about proposing restrictions in peace time.

There is one group of workers who are directly and permanently concerned with the protection of the realm and that is

4. Eric Wigham, *Strikes and the Government*, op. cit., p. 91.

the members of the armed forces. In Britain such persons are not employees in the normal sense. They do not enter into contracts of employment but either enlist for, or until 1957 were conscripted into, the forces for a specified period of time. Although individual members of the armed forces may retain their preservice union membership, no attempt has ever been made in Britain by trade unions to represent the interests of such members while in the forces; still less to establish a trade union organization for serving soldiers. The traditional and established view has always been that the very nature, as well as the effectiveness, of the armed forces is dependent on the maintenance of military discipline, requiring unquestioned obedience to superiors at all times. This precludes trade unionism amongst members of the armed forces, since trade unionism necessarily involves the questioning of authority. Since the Second World War, however, trade union membership has been permitted in the German armed forces, and some 100,000 soldiers are members of the Public Services and Transport Workers Union, which negotiates on their behalf with the military authorities. Soldier members of the union elect representatives to the local branch in whose area they are stationed.[5] It would appear, then, that union membership is not incompatible with the maintenance of the armed forces, any more than it is incompatible with the maintenance of a police force.

But if this is accepted it raises the question whether the right to strike itself might be, or ought to be, granted to members of the armed forces at least in peacetime. In support of such a radical step it might be argued that, since the right to strike is a fundamental right, no group of persons should be deprived of that right unless the exercise of that right can under certain strict and specified conditions be shown to be a direct and serious threat to the lives and safety of others, e.g. a strike of seamen at sea. The armed services in peacetime would not qualify for exemption on

5. Letters to author from Dr R. Vollmer, Embassy of the Federal Republic of Germany in London, 13 September 1976, and from the International Department of Gewerkschaft Öffentliche Dienste Transport und Verkehr, 17 July 1979.

this ground; indeed a strike in the armed forces would have less impact on the lives of other members of the community than a strike of almost any other group of workers. In peacetime the armed forces provide almost no direct services at all to the community: in wartime, of course, such strikes would be banned. But, even if one accepts that the right to strike ought only to be restricted to prevent a serious threat to life or safety, the conclusion with regard to the armed forces remains open to objection. Firstly it makes a rigid and unrealistic distinction between the position of the armed forces in peacetime and wartime. The degree of effectiveness of a country's armed forces in peacetime is a highly important and relevant factor in international relations. A strike-ridden army may well constitute a serious threat by reducing the country's military credibility and encouraging foreign adventurism. More specifically the position of the IRA in Northern Ireland would be immensely strengthened if the armed forces there were to strike in support of grievances resulting from their employment on their dangerous and unpleasant duties. Secondly, the armed forces are called in to deal with emergencies both at home and overseas and must be ready to depart at a few hours' notice, without any regard to their own interests or commitments, the dangers of their mission or their reward – all matters which a union might well wish to make subject to strike action or threat. But most important of all, in this context, the armed forces are themselves used to run essential services, and in the last resort to deal with serious breakdowns of law and order resulting from major industrial strikes. It is difficult to believe that these tasks could be, or would be, adequately carried out by men who were themselves organized in a trade union with strike powers. Strong moral pressure would undoubtably be exercised by striking 'fellow unionists' to dissuade them from acting as strike-breakers. Politically it would be an impossible position if the Government of the day had to secure the approval of armed service union leaders before it could carry out its responsibility to maintain essential supplies and services during an industrial dispute. It is in large part because the Government can rely on the use of the armed services in such situations that it is able to accept that civilian workers in essential services should be permitted to strike. It is, therefore, in the interests of trade unions themselves that the armed forces should not be drawn into the industrial disputes' arena.[6]

2. Maintenance of the rule of law

The right of citizens to have the protection of the rule of law covers such basic areas as the maintenance of order, the protection of persons and property, and access to the legal system. These areas may be affected by strikes either directly through the threatening attitude of strikers, or indirectly through the strike action of workers themselves employed to provide the necessary services needed to maintain the rule of law.

Only those who see strikes in class-war terms, when all that matters is winning, will accept that strikers are entitled to use any means to beat their class enemy, including the use of physical violence and the destruction of property; unless, of course, the employers themselves have initiated a campaign of violence against the strikers, which the authorities failed or refused to put down (as happened extensively in the United States right down to the 1930s). Striker violence and destruction, rare in itself in Britain, is still more rarely perpetrated against persons or property not directly involved in the dispute concerned. Where it does occur it is likely to assume the form, not of a riot or rampage, as in the past, but of coercive mass secondary picketing, as in the 1972 miners' national strike. Since, under any but the most extreme or unusual circumstances, no grounds can be adduced to justify strikers using violence or threats of intimidation against fellow workers who do not wish to come out on strike, it is apparent that such action is completely indefensible when practised

6. The West German Public Services and Transport Workers Union states that though the union claims that soldiers, along with other civil servants, have a right to strike, the prevailing legal view is that civil servants do not have such a right. The union itself has included a self-limitation in its constitution (article 19) which provides that policemen, firemen and soldiers will not be called out on strike. Letter to author, 17 July 1979.

against those *not* party to the dispute. I have a right to be protected against those who would forcibly seek to thrust their troubles on my shoulders and compel me, against my wishes, to fight for their cause, whether by boycotting their employer or by preventing me working for my own. The right not to be coerced is not incompatible with the right to strike; on the contrary, it is the foundation on which the latter stands.[7]

It is even more immediately apparent that coercive action against outside workers undermines the basis of the case for sympathetic strike action. That case rests on the principle of working-class solidarity and sympathy. It takes the form of an appeal for help from those in danger of losing, in a dispute of such general importance or particular concern that others ought to come to their aid. But there is no question here of those calling for help having a moral right to it, in the sense that other workers have a duty to respond. This would only be the case if specific ties of mutual obligation had been established between respective groups of workers. In all other cases the most that could be claimed was a moral right to be heard and a moral duty of others to listen; but it rests with the bodies appealed to, to decide for themselves whether to assist, and if so what form such assistance should take. Sympathetic strike action is indeed rare compared with the gifts of money to strike funds. Nevertheless the principle of the right of appeal and of a duty to give sympathetic consideration to appeals is an important one and finds its most impressive expression in the 1926 General Strike in support of the miners. But those who claim the right to appeal for help cannot validly claim the right to use coercion either against those who fail to respond or against those they made no appeal to. One might well hazard that those who claim the right to use coercion to secure the desired compliance of other workers would not accept a reciprocal right against themselves, though it is apparent that some groups of workers are far less vulnerable to counter-attack than those who are the targets of attack.

7. A survey conducted by Market and Opinion Research in July 1980 showed two thirds of union members in favour of a ban on secondary picketing. *Sunday Times*, 31 August 1980.

Coercive picketing is both legally forbidden and morally condemned by trade unions, but that does not prevent its occurrence. The body responsible for ensuring that the law is complied with is the police. Policemen in Britain are forbidden by the Police Act 1919 from belonging to any trade union or political association, and though not legally debarred from taking strike action, are liable to dismissal if they do so. However, the Police Federation increasingly acts as a trade union and there is strong support within the Federation for the acquisition of strike powers. In North America police strikes are a familiar, if unwelcome, phenomenon. While there is clear evidence of increases in property crimes, including muggings, during police strikes it is not apparent that strike action necessarily causes more harm to the public than other public forms of collective expressions of police resentment and grievance – working to rule, absenteeism, go-slows, etc. Members of the public, especially the old and the alone, may, however, suffer considerably from apprehension of the dangers to themselves when the custodians of law and order 'down tools'. There is something deeply disquieting in seeing on the TV screen picketing policemen being arrested by National Guardsmen and locked up in their own jail for committing offences of violence. Furthermore the possibility that the police might, instead of policing a strike, actually join it, cannot be ruled out. In the Winnipeg General Strike in 1919 the policemen voted to join the strike, only remaining on duty at the request of the strike committee. In community terms it seems highly undesirable that the public should be confronted with police strikes, since such strikes are very liable to give rise to just those disorders the police are there to prevent.

Two other groups of workers with major reponsibilities for the protection of life and property are those in the fire and ambulance services. A strong case could be made for forbidding such workers, along with policemen, from striking altogether, in return for guarantees about binding arbitration awards from independent tribunals, which would be expressly recognized as not bound by the requirements of Government pay policy. In the absence of such an agreement with the fire service and ambulancemen's unions, the public have a right to expect such workers to act with full regard to the responsibility they have undertaken for the protection of life and property: a responsibility which is indeed much more direct and immediate than that of the police in this respect. This end might be secured by a code of practice on the following lines:

1. Recognition of the overriding claims of the right of the public to the protection of life and property.
2. Strike action not to be undertaken except as a last resort.
3. Independent arbitration with binding awards.
4. Recognition of the duty to maintain an agreed minimum service at all times.
5. Acceptance of the Government's right to take steps to secure additional services (e.g. the armed forces), without withdrawal of union-guaranteed cover, if the minimum cover available is less than adequate.

Similar codes of practice might be applied in other limited areas of employment directly concerned with the maintenance of the rule of law, e.g. prison officers or the staffs of the Courts.

Such schemes would be acceptable only if the Government were able to demonstrate convincingly that it was guided solely by the need to provide adequate services, not with breaking the strike. Guarantees to this end might be secured through the services of the Trades Union Congress.

3. Protection of the right to work

One must accept as a necessary price of the right to strike some curtailment of the right to work of those in jobs adversely affected by somebody else's strike (e.g. suppliers of their components or users of their products). The case for asserting a right of such workers not to be prevented from working by coercive secondary picketing has been set out above (pp. 132–3), and that case applies with equal force to coercive secondary picketing against those supplying firms on strike with goods or services. Indeed, there seems no moral reason to justify any group of striking workers *deliberately* depriving other workers not directly involved in the dispute of their right to work in order to further their own strike interests. The right not to be stopped from working against one's will by outside strikers is as basic as the right not to be coerced into striking. But while the principle at issue is clear, the means for its practical realization are not easy to discern. Since, however, picketing in hard-fought disputes is commonly associated with hot tempers and the possibility of violence, and since it is in just such disputes that secondary picketing is normally undertaken, there is a case for prohibiting secondary picketing altogether, while leaving open the opportunity for sympathetic strike action.

Quite different problems arise with those unable to work, or dependent for a living income on supplementary benefit payments. The old, the widowed, the members of large families, the single-parent families, include the poorest, the most disadvantaged, the most inadequate and inarticulate members of the community. Those responsible for making the welfare payments on which such persons depend can never justify strike action which would cut them off from their means of survival. The crucial test, 'What if it were me, or my widowed mother, or forsaken daughter?' will show the road of duty, unless some alternative means of payment can be provided or secured.

4. Provision of essential supplies and services

Strikers and employers are in no position to claim the right to fight out their disputes without regard to the impact on the lives of other members of the community. Nor is it an adequate response for the striker to show that he and his family, equally with the non-striker, suffer from the ill-effects of the stoppage, since he brings these burdens on himself of his own free will in the hope of later benefits, while the latter have the burdens imposed on them with no expectation of compensating gains, indeed often the contrary prospect of higher prices or taxes. The needs of society in major strike outbreaks cannot be ascertained by reference to what different groups of strikers are each willing to put up with in their particular strike. Men are often ready to take risks with themselves which they have no right to require others to take, and which no Government has the right to accept for its citizens.

The first need that has to be met is for food. The only form of strike likely to produce hunger, as distinct from shortages of particular foods, is a prolonged road haulage, dockers' or seamen's strike. In such an event the Government would be bound at some stage to use troops to maintain essential supplies. For their part, the strikers themselves would have a direct obligation to ensure that nobody suffered severely from the food shortage they had caused. This would require them not to hinder the Government's emergency operations and, if these broke down or were inadequate, to make their own services available for this purpose. Successive British Governments have adequately coped with this fortunately rare situation without the public suffering more than inconvenience. In general strikes it has been customary both for strikers and anti-strike volunteers to provide their own separate organizations for the distribution of food and the maintenance of essential services, acting in conjunction with the public authorities. The strikers' right is not the right to secure capitulation under threat of causing dire suffering, but the more limited right characteristic of most strike action to draw attention to their grievances and cause inconvenience or dislocation sufficient to induce their employers to negotiate a settlement. Strikers ought, therefore, to accept the right of the Government to maintain a minimum level of services through the use of the armed or other services. Where, as in the case of electricity generation, such resources are inadequate to maintain an acceptable minimum level the authorities might consider seeking 'no strike' guarantees from the unions concerned, in return for Government guarantees of fair treatment, as suggested above for the police and ambulance services.

More difficult problems arise with transport and communications, including post and telephones, which employ very large groups of workers, many of whom are lowly paid. With the exceptions of parts of the road haulage industry, and the key group of petrol and oil tanker drivers, such workers in Britain are all employed in the public sector of the economy and the services they provide are monopoly services which cannot be met from other sources. Fortunately, however, the withdrawal of such services causes dislocation and inconvenience to individuals rather than direct harm. Though such strikes may do serious harm to the economy, the same is true of any major stoppage. There appears to be no grounds, therefore, for treating strikes in these sectors any differently from strikes elsewhere. It is worth noting that Government concern to maintain overseas confidence and the strength of sterling has led to the adoption of wages policies which have resulted in some of the most serious national disputes experienced in recent years. This problem is discussed below (pp. 143–7).

The third group of essential services are the health services which exist to meet what has come to be recognized as perhaps the most fundamental of man's social rights – the right to medical treatment for sickness, injury or disease. The health services exist to save life, remove suffering and prevent disability, and the service they provide in modern Western society is more crucial to more people than any other. The question of strike action in this area thus raises issues which are qualitatively different from those raised elsewhere. The 1977 firemen's strike in Britain lasted two months, and while millions of extra pounds of property was destroyed, the extent of physical suffering or injury caused was relatively small: whether anyone died as the result of the strike is a matter of conjecture. If the hospitals in Britain had been totally closed down for the same period, hundreds, perhaps thousands of persons would have died or had their lives shortened, while tens of thousands would have endured great suffering and suffered serious disability. As far as the members of the medical profession themselves are concerned, there can be no doubt that the nature of their calling as doctors, surgeons and nurses imposes on them a moral duty never to strike or engage in any action designed to reduce the level of service provided, *no matter how deep or bitter their sense of grievance.* Even if their grievance is at policies or practices which, in their view, seriously and adversely affect the service itself, they should confine themselves to forms of demonstration and protest which do not adversely affect the health and welfare of their patients or patients-to-come; recognizing that precisely because of the crucial nature of their work to the public, the public are capable of being aroused in support of their just cause, if just it be.

In the case of the hospital service, however, it has been made readily apparent that their effective operation is dependent on the work of tens of thousands of non-medical staff, many of whom are very lowly paid. Is it reasonable to hold that part-time ward orderlies or cleaners have an equal obligation with the doctors and nurses not to withdraw their labour? The union answer in 1979 was 'No', but in their strike the unions accepted that they ought not to close down the hospitals. Instead they provided a minimum staff cover, adequate in their view for the admission of emergency patients. This is not a satisfactory or acceptable position. One cannot admit the right or the capacity of trade unions to decide who shall, and who shall not, be admitted for treatment. Unions ought to accept the need to maintain a fully adequate level of service, through some combination of union-provided emergency staff plus volunteers, possibly with payments for emergency staff work made over to the union for distribution as strike pay. Such arrangements could certainly reduce the impact of the strike both in terms of human suffering and in terms of dislocation, but not significantly, as emergency and volunteer arrangements are necessarily second-best expedients. Indeed such arrangements need not be disadvantageous as they could be expected to increase public sympathy for the union's cause. Sympathy though, as union organizers of the lowly paid know only too well, is not enough. It needs to be backed up by machinery designed to ensure that the Government of the day does not take advantage of arrangements

139

made to secure the rights of patients for questionable purposes of its own. If the public are to secure special service in strikes from unions in the health sector they must be prepared to pay for it through some form of guarantee for the implementation of an independent review board's findings on low wages in that sector.

A final word must be said about the impact of strikes on the right of parents and children to education. Though the withdrawal of education facilities has no physical adverse effects, its seriousness cannot be doubted. In some cases it may result in children failing to achieve the academic standards they require to qualify for further education or for particular jobs, to their permanent disadvantage. In others, children with working mothers, or with only one parent, may be forced to spend strike days on the streets, or their parents to take time off from work. These two objections might be met if teachers (a) took steps to ensure that special tuition were provided during the strike for those shortly taking exams, and after the strike, for those whose education had suffered and (b) adequate advance notice of a strike were given and an emergency care service provided for young school children who could not otherwise be looked after. Such measures to reduce the most serious adverse effects of strike action by teachers would not, however, meet the objection that strike action is subversive of the teacher-pupil relationship, based as it is on the twin concepts of service and concern. These concepts are fundamental to teaching as a profession and require that teachers do not treat the strike as simply a weapon available to secure their demands, but rather as a last resort means of protest against, on the one hand, a refusal by the authorities to submit their claims to arbitration or give effect to arbitration awards; and, on the other, against policies which undermine the education service itself.

5. Maintenance of freedom of expression

The exercise of the right to strike rarely trespasses on the right to freedom of expression. The mass media, in particular, freely gives rein to anti-strike feelings, often without any serious attempt to ascertain or explain the striker's point of view. Freedom of expression is likely to become an issue only where clashes arise between strikers and non-strikers, or in a strike of workers employed in the mass media. With regard to the first it is wrong to think of strikers either as a united band of militants dedicated to the realization of their rightful objective, or as industrial soldiers unquestioningly following their leaders into battle. The whole conduct and purpose of the strike is a matter of continuous discussion and dispute, at home, in the pub and on the picket line. Strike leaders, union officials, as well as management, will all be subject to criticism, both by those who voted for strike action and by those who voted against. But, since both groups are bound by the original strike decision, both are required to ensure they do not act in ways contrary to that decision. The strikers who opposed the original strike decision may not publicly campaign for its reversal by publishing leaflets, calling meetings or giving interviews to the press, since such actions will serve to undermine both the authority of the strike meeting's decision and the effectiveness of the strike action undertaken.

Different considerations arise for workers who do not join the strike, where no obligation to do so can be established (see pp. 91–106 above). Such workers are clearly not restricted in the exercise of their right of freedom of expression in the ways mentioned above for strikers. On the contrary, they are entitled to do all they think necessary to put their own anti-strike case to the strikers and the public at large. In practice, however, this is rarely done. Non-strikers are reluctant to organize themselves, to produce anti-strike leaflets, hold anti-strike meetings, or set up anti-picket lines. On the contrary, non-strikers are usually on the defensive, anxious to retain a low profile and to make no trouble for themselves. They feel and act as individuals, and as such are vulnerable to collective pressure and to the accusation of sacrificing group interest to narrow personal greed. If non-strikers were to take concerted action to vindicate their position, clashes with irate strikers could be expected.

The threat to freedom of expression presented by the prospect

141

of strike action by workers engaged in the mass communications industries, on the other hand, is more apparent than real, unless there were to be a total shut-down of all sources of news and information. As long as alternative sources were available a strike, even of all newspapers *or* all television workers, though inconvenient and annoying, could not be said to present a challenge to democratic government and democratic society. A total shutdown of both is virtually inconceivable except in the context of a general strike.

GOVERNMENT RIGHTS AND DUTIES

It has been my concern in the preceding discussion to establish the impact of the exercise of the right to strike by particular groups of workers upon the basic rights persons have as members of a political community. Where a conflict of rights was revealed resolution was sought by attempting to establish the minimum legal restrictions that ought to be placed on, or the minimum moral restrictions which ought to be accepted by, the workers and unions concerned if the minimum legitimate rights of members of the community, and especially those of the least privileged, are to be adequately secured.

The discussion of the conflict between the right to strike and other basic rights has brought out the crucial role of the Government in such conflicts. It is to the key question of the rights and duties of the Government in relation to the strike that we must now turn.

The problem can best be examined in the context of two major trends which are still continuing:

1. The steady increase since the beginning of the century in the proportion of the working population employed by public authorities.
2. The rapid growth over the past forty years in the responsibility assumed by the Government for running the economy and in the powers exercised for that purpose.

Both of these developments are common to the whole Western world and both have been strongly advocated and supported by the British Labour and trade union movements. What was not readily appreciated was their possible impact on the right to strike. That impact has been most noticeable within the public sector itself. On the one hand, with the widespread extension of unionization within the public service, and with the erosion of the conception that striking by non-industrial public servants was both a disciplinary offence and contrary to the spirit of the public service, there has been an effective assertion of a right to strike for all public employees.[8] On the other hand, pay settlements in the public sector are now so important, both in themselves and for their impact on the private sector, that Governments are increasingly forced into taking up bargaining stances which themselves give rise to the threat or practice of strike action. The general public today is more likely to be seriously inconvenienced by the strikes of workers in the public service than in private industry. It is difficult to see how this situation could have been avoided, except by the enactment of legislation prohibiting strike action by non-industrial public service workers – legislation which would have been bitterly contested, and rightly contested, by the whole trade union movement.

We now have a situation where the British Government holds itself, and is itself held, responsible for the management of an economy, a large part of which is in its direct employ or under its

8. An indication of the extent to which the climate of opinion and practice has changed can be judged from this quotation from the speech of the Labour Attorney General in 1946 when moving the second reading of the Trades Disputes and Trade Union Bill – 'The 1927 Act did not forbid civil servants to strike, and nothing that we propose to do now will make it more legal than it is today for civil servants to take strike action . . . I take the opportunity of making it quite clear that this Government, like any Government as an employer would feel perfectly free to take any disciplinary action that any strike situation that might develop demanded.' Quoted by Marc Somerhausen, 'The Right to Strike in the Public Service', lecture given at the XVII Congress of the Public Services International in Stockholm, 24 to 29 August 1964.

direct control. In such circumstances it is inevitable that Government economic policies, whether Labour or Conservative, should commonly give rise, especially in the recurring periods of stress and difficulty, to conflicts with the public service unions as the Government seeks to give effect to wages and prices policies in the large area immediately subject to its direction. The right of the Government of the day to seek to implement its economic policies cannot be gainsaid, but what of the union's right to strike where those policies include a wage freeze or wage ceiling? The Labour Government in 1966 passed legislation making trade unions liable to prosecution if they took strike action to force employers to make wage increases above the levels permitted by legislation. Conservative legislation on wage control between 1972 and 1974 made trade unions liable to prosecution for breaches of the Act, but, unlike the former Labour legislation, did not make strikes intended to encourage breaches of the legislation specific grounds for prosecution. In neither instance were any prosecutions instigated, although a considerable number of stoppages took place; suggesting that the Governments concerned concluded that more industrial unrest and more injury to the Governments' objectives would be caused by operating the sanctions than by keeping them in reserve. More recently the Callaghan administration threatened and operated sanctions solely against employers who, under threat of strike action, gave wage increases in excess of those laid down by the Government. The latter policy is clearly inequitable; justifiable, if at all, in the narrowest terms of political expediency, against what must have appeared to the Labour Government as economically the weaker and politically the less relevant of the two sides of industry.

While there can be no objection to any Government pursuing policies of wage restraint in order to realize its economic objectives, the use of sanction-backed legislation prohibiting strikes in support of wage claims beyond pay policy limits may be open to serious objection on both moral and political grounds.

Moral Grounds

1. *If the method used is objectionable in itself* – involving a major restriction of the right to strike in a central area of established and legitimate union concern.
2. *If there is a high risk of objectionable consequences* – the likelihood that at some stage the use of sanctions would result in the imprisonment of strikers or union officials.
3. *If making the law effective requires the application of an objectionable level of sanctions* – strike prohibition is never effective in a democratic society: the price of effectiveness is the imposition of an authoritarian regime.
4. (a) *If the authorities are highly selective in determining which offenders are prosecuted, deliberately ignoring most known offenders and choosing candidates for prosecution on grounds of political expediency, not moral culpability* – this was the position in both World Wars during the period when strikes generally were banned.
   or
   (b) *If no prosecutions are ever made in spite of many breaches of the legislation* – this was the position under wage restraint legislation operative in 1966–8 and 1972–4.

Political Grounds

1. *If the legislation does not work* – it is impossible to determine whether the existence of sanctions against strikes was a material factor in holding back wage increases in 1966–8 and 1972–4.
2. *If its purpose may be effectively secured without sanction-backed legislation* – voluntary wage restraint worked between 1976 and 1978.
3. *If the purpose may be effectively secured by other methods not involving the use of sanction-backed legislation* – a wide range of economic, fiscal and taxation methods are available to the Government to deal with the consequences of wage inflation.

4. *If the effect of operating the sanctions is to undermine the purpose of the policy it is designed to serve* – the Industrial Relations Act 1971, designed to reduce the level of strikes, was itself a major cause of the heavy rise in strike activity between 1971 and 1974.
5. *If the effect of operating the policy is to create a high level of political or social unrest* – as with the Conservative Government's sanction-backed wages policy between 1972 and 1974.

It is important to note that while political arguments may be levelled against giving effect to these moral objections, moral arguments will normally reinforce the political objections. However, the fourth moral ground 4(b) will appear as a political commendation as long as the broad purposes of the legislation concerned are being realized, or as long as more persons abide by the legislation in spite of no offenders being prosecuted than would do so in the absence of such legislation. Where political objections reinforce moral objections, as in the case of wage restraint, the grounds for asserting that the right to strike has been wrongly restricted are very strong. The moral case against Government intervention is even stronger if the restriction on striking is made general, and the reasons given for enforcing it are the promotion of economic production and welfare, since such reasons may be invoked at almost any time. This was a policy pursued by the Labour Government between 1945 and 1951 and is open to moral objections on grounds 1, 2, 3 and 4(a). Politically very similar arguments can be levelled to those set out in 1, 2, and 3, but the strongest objection is 4 since, as soon as the authorities used sanctions against 1,700 striking gas workers in the autumn of 1950, the whole edifice of wage restraint (the pivot of the Government's economic policy) collapsed and the Order prohibiting strikes had to be withdrawn (see note 2, p. 128). Total bans on strikes and lock-outs introduced to promote production are open to further moral and political objections.

Moral Objections

1. Bans will operate against strikes designed to secure the removal of barriers to increased production or of conditions which are a cause of reduced production.
2. Bans will operate against strikes where strike action is the only effective way of securing prompt redress to serious legitimate grievances.
3. Bans will take away from workers their main weapon of industrial struggle while leaving employers with their main weapon – the sack or threat of sacking.

Political Objections

1. The operation of sanctions against any group of strikers will almost certainly cause more harm to production than the strike in which they are engaged.
2. The ban may lead to workers adopting other means of expressing their grievances which cause greater harm to production, e.g. collective operation of go-slow policy or individual resort to absenteeism.

In my view the moral and political objections to a general ban on strikes are so strong that it cannot be justified even in war time.

Is the position significantly altered if, instead of a legal proscription on strike action, restrictions are imposed which require certain conditions to be met before strike action is permitted? Two major requirements for strike action may be considered – arbitration or conciliation requirements, and voting requirements.

Compulsory arbitration machinery in this country has been used extensively in conjunction with complete strike prohibition, but it would be possible to require that strikes would be permitted only as a last resort after arbitration and against an unacceptable award. To judge by the polls conducted by Gallup between 1966 and 1974 this was the preferred choice of roughly 40 per cent of the British public, with 25 per cent supporting compulsory arbitration and 25 per cent the status quo.[9] Such a restriction would certainly be a less severe limitation on the right to strike than outright banning and would be one which would have met the requirements of many nineteenth-century trade unionists who argued that the strike weapon was necessary precisely because there was no independent wage determination machinery available. However, if one is to eliminate a high risk of morally objectionable consequences, and the near certainty of political and social chaos, it would be necessary to restrict these requirements to national wage claims and national stoppages, while recognizing that such stoppages are widely accepted as much less damaging economically than the thousands of unofficial and unconstitutional stoppages. With this major qualification there appears no overriding *moral* objection to only allowing strike action against arbitration awards, provided that agreement can be reached on the constitution of adequate independent arbitration for every industry. There are, however, strong political reasons for not introducing such a provision into British industrial life, in view of the bitter opposition of the unions. Conceptually, too, there is something 'odd' about forbidding all national stoppages except those against independent arbitration awards, unless independent arbitration is seen, not as a means of determining what is fair, but as an assessment of the price at which a strike

9. *Gallup Political Index*	Sept. 1966	Sept. 1968	Sept. 1969	Sept. 1974
Which of these arguments do you support:				
1. The right to strike is one of the essential freedoms of workers in a democracy.	25%	25%	20%	25%
2. Strikes should be made illegal and pay disputes should be referred to compulsory arbitration.	28%	26%	26%	24%
3. Workers should be allowed to strike when arbitration has failed to bring about an agreement acceptable to workers.	40%	39%	40%	41%
4. Don't know.	10%	13%	14%	11%

can be avoided. Strike action would indicate that the arbitrators made a mistake and gave too low an award.

A power to require unions to take a strike ballot before embarking on strike action was included in the Conservative ill-fated Industrial Relations Act 1971. A strong case can be made in terms of democratic theory for unions not embarking on major, as distinct from token, national stoppages unless they have clear evidence of majority backing from their members. It does not follow from this, however, that a Government would be justified in requiring unions to conduct postal ballots for this purpose, any more than one would want to require that the Government itself conducts a referendum before giving effect to any major legislative proposal. Intervention of this kind is objectionable since it involves interference with the way trade unions conduct their affairs. On the political level it is interesting to note that the Conservative Party and Government has moved to the more defensible position of encouraging instead of requiring unions to conduct strike ballots.[10]

The general conclusion I would draw from this discussion is that the role of Government in a democratic society with regard to strikes should be confined to the provision of facilities for conciliation and arbitration, intervening in major disputes to secure a settlement, and taking steps to safeguard the basic rights of individuals.

In the light of this discussion we can now turn to the question of whether trade unions are entitled to use the strike weapon against the Government. It is necessary to make a sharp distinction at the very beginning between *protest strikes* designed to draw attention to the extent and depth of feeling existing against a particular Government law, policy, or action, and *coercive strikes* designed to force the Government to change that policy. In a democratic society any group or organization of persons is entitled to demonstrate its opposition to the Government, as long as

10. The Opinion and Market Research survey showed six out of seven union members in favour of no strikes being called until there had been a postal ballot of the union members concerned. The *Sunday Times*, 31 August 1980.

its direct purpose or effect is not to make it impossible or hazardous for the Government to promote its policies and activities. No threat to democratic government of democratic principles, for example, was presented by the hundreds of thousands of trade unionists who staged a one-day strike against the Conservative Industrial Relations Bill in 1970. Demonstration protest strikes are by their nature invariably short, causing at worst only very temporary inconvenience or dislocation. The only valid objection that could be raised in democratic terms against political protest strikes is not against their staging but their purpose. Thus a strike in support of the National Front policy of forcible repatriation of immigrants might be objected to on the grounds that, while the strikers had a legal and constitutional right to strike, they were morally wrong to do so in furtherance of such a morally objectionable purpose.

Quite different considerations arise with regard to coercive strikes designed to force the Government's hand. In constitutional terms there would appear to be no justification in a democratic society for strike action designed to coerce the elected Government or to frustrate its policies. But this is an oversimplification since it fails to take account of the realities of democratic government on the one hand, and the nature, purposes and possible effects of the coercive strike action on the other. Democratic government, as practised, does not match the high principles of classic liberal democratic theory as expressed by John Stuart Mill or T. H. Green. It is a muddy world where the rhetoric of the popular will and the national interest is all too often used to cover up shabby deals and shoddy compromises with powerful groups or favoured interests. Quite apart from criminal corruption, and its near-criminal relatives, behind-the-scenes activity by organized groups and institutions aimed at influencing or altering the direction of government policy for the benefit of the group or institution concerned is a widespread and recognized feature of the modern Western political process. Powerful financial and business interests, in particular, negotiate with Government authorities from a position of strength which enables them to extract concessions and advantages, often without the public being aware of what has occurred. But the spectacle of giant multinational firms threatening to shut down their plants in Britain unless the Government hands over huge financial grants seems to arouse less adverse public criticism and concern than the prospect of strikes directed at securing changes in Government policy detrimental to union interests. A poll conducted in 1975 showed 57 per cent opposing, and only 17 per cent supporting, strikes 'to get the Government to change its policies'.[11]

Coercive strikes directed against the Government may be divided into two broad groups: strikes in furtherance of central union interests and objectives ('economic' strikes), and strikes in furtherance of specifically political objectives ('political' strikes). Each category may be further divided according to whether the strike is called by one union (or group of unions in one firm or industry), or by the whole trade union movement.

ECONOMIC STRIKES AGAINST THE GOVERNMENT

For analytical purposes it is helpful to start by looking at general strikes called for economic purposes, since we are able to discuss the issue against the most celebrated of all general strikes, the 1926 General Strike called by the T.U.C. in support of the miners. No British Government since the Baldwin Government in 1926 has faced the threat of a general strike. The T.U.C. rejected calls for strike action against the Trades Disputes Act 1927, and the Industrial Relations Act 1971, and its response to the imprisonment of the 'Pentonville Five' in 1972 was a call for a one-day national protest strike, which never materialized as the men were released before the date fell due. It is apparent that only the most

---

11. *Public's Message: We Back the Constitution.* Results of a survey for Aims of Freedom and Enterprise carried out by N.O.P. Market Research Ltd., November 1975. The difficulty of drawing clear and firm conclusions from the poll is indicated by the fact that as many people expressed disagreement with strikes 'to get shorter working hours' (66 per cent) as with strikes 'to get Parliament to change a law' (65 per cent), though the former is a long-established and accepted trade union objective.

extreme and extraordinary situation would now persuade the British trade union movement to call a coercive general strike. Since the credibility of such a serious venture turns on the prospect of securing overwhelming support, the issue can only arise where there is already a deep and widespread sense of intense grievance. Moreover, given the controversy and disquiet surrounding general strikes, British trade unions would only consider embarking on such a course with the greatest reluctance and for the sole purpose of securing the remedy of the grievance concerned. The last thing Western trade union leaders want is embroilment in a political or constitutional crisis.[12] A brief glance at the British General Strike of May 1926 is revealing in this respect. The positions taken up by the various parties on the eve of the strike turned on their attitude to the Report of the Samuel Commission set up by the Government in 1925 to inquire into the coal industry, and were roughly as follows:

Figure 4 (a) 1926 General Strike – positions of parties to the dispute

Samuel Commission	Owners	Miners	Government
Agreement on reorganization of coal industry *then*	No reorganization	Reorganization of industry	Reorganization of industry
wage cuts*	Immediate wage cuts	No wage cuts	Immediate wage cuts
Maintenance of national wage agreements	District wage agreements	National wage agreements	National wage agreements
No increase in hours (fixed by law)	Increase in hours	No increase in hours	Increase in hours

* Miners' wages had been subsidized since August 1925 by the Government at a cost of £23 million.

12. This would not necessarily be true of the Communist leaders of the French and Italian trade union movements; but such movements are both weaker than, and different in many ways from, the British trade union movement.

The T.U.C. accepted that some wage cuts would almost certainly be necessary and were prepared to negotiate a settlement based on the Samuel Commission Report. The cost of avoiding the General Strike, or of meeting the T.U.C.'s requirements once it had started, can be represented as follows:

Figure 4 (a) 1926 General Strike – cost of meeting T.U.C. minimum requirements

Cost to Government	Cost to Coal-owners	Cost to Miners
Payment of temporary subsidy during period of negotiations	No immediate reduction in wages. Likelihood that negotiated wage cuts would be less than the owners could impose. Retention of national wage rates.	Likelihood that wages would be cut within a few months.
Abandonment of proposal to increase hours of work.	No increase in hours of work.	
Forcing owners to accept reorganization of industry.	Imposition of reorganization.	
Forcing owners to withdraw lock-out notices.*		

* The coal-owners had locked out the miners before the General Strike began.

Given the close association of the Government with the mining industry, the intransigent attitude of the coal-owners, and the suffering which would result from the imposition of the owners' lock-out terms on the already depressed miners, the decision of the T.U.C. to intervene in the dispute was fully justified and its proposals were moderate. Indeed, it can be argued that they were too moderate, or at least too limited, and that, both in terms of social justice and of expediency (the need to secure the miners'

support for T.U.C. proposals), they should have included a demand
for a continuance of the Government subsidy until such time as the
reorganized industry was itself able to meet the cost of paying
reasonable wages. Even with such a provision the proposals would
not have placed an unreasonably heavy or impossible charge on
the country's financial resources.[13]

The only question at issue is whether the T.U.C. were justified
in threatening, or in undertaking, a general strike to secure their
moderate proposals. The issue was and still is a matter of con-
tention, where judgement is made more difficult by the com-
plexities of the developing situation and the ineptitude and
confusion of the actors on all sides. At one level one may argue that
the Government's failure to provide a ready response to the
T.U.C.'s proposals, and its precipitate breaking off of negotiations,
justified the strike action taken. There was no threat to democratic or constitutional government, since those who led the
strike had no intentions beyond the realization of their limited
proposals for the coal industry. The implementation of these proposals would not have imposed an impossibly heavy burden on
the Exchequer, nor would they have undermined the ability of the
Government to realize its policy objectives, or constitute a rad-
ically new and unwarranted interference with the rights of
private industry. Against this, it may be asserted that the authority of the Government was seriously challenged by the threat of
strike action on a national scale, involving as it did the assertion
by the unions of quasi-governmental authority during the course
of the strike. Only the capitulation of the T.U.C. had prevented
this challenge from assuming the form of open confrontation. Even

13. Mr Churchill's 1925 Budget (drawn up before any question of coal
subsidy had arisen) showed a projected surplus of income over expenditure
of £26 million − £24 million of which he devoted to reducing the standard
rate of income tax, by 6d in the £ (costing £32 million in a full year). He was
able to meet the cost of the coal subsidy without increasing taxes, or dip-
ping into the sinking fund for the redemption of the National Debt, by using
£10,000,000 of his projected surplus for 1926/7 to replace the £10,000,000
borrowed from the supply fund for subsidy purposes. (*The Annual Register*,
1925 and 1926).

if the T.U.C.'s proposals were reasonable, and the Government's response open to severe criticism, that did not mean that the trade unions were entitled to bring the country to a halt in order to force the Government to adopt policies to which it was opposed.

In terms of democratic theory, as distinct from Marxist theory, the case for the 1926 General Strike is at best a doubtful one. That example shows that a sympathetic strike by the whole trade union movement will necessarily assume for the Government the form of a challenge to its authority, irrespective of the limited purposes of the strike leaders themselves. That is not to say that a general strike is in principle unjustified (still less that it should be legally proscribed as in the Trades Disputes Act 1927), but only that, given the necessarily political nature of the challenge, it would require a direct political threat to democratic practices or to the rights of trade unions to exist and operate to be justifiable. The former is discussed below (pp. 159–61). The strict requirements of the latter can be gauged from the fact that the trade unions themselves did not regard the restrictions imposed on their activities by either the Trade Disputes Act 1927 or the Industrial Relations Act 1971 as grounds for general coercive industrial action.

The great difference between an economic general strike and an ordinary economic strike directed against the Government is that the latter is not in itself a direct challenge to the Government's authority to run the country or a possible threat to the constitution. On the other hand strikes of this character, unlike general strikes, are a quite familiar feature of the modern industrial scene. Before discussing specific problems it is necessary to touch on the situation created by the emergence of the Government as both the largest single employer of labour directly on the one hand and the indirect controller and financier of much of the public sector of employment on the other. In general it is accepted and acceptable that labour relations in the public sector should be treated on the same basis as those in private industry with regard to the exercise of the right to strike. However, the fact that the money to meet the cost of strike-backed union demands has to come directly from public funds (i.e. in large part from the taxes levied on other workers) does mean that there is a moral obligation on the part of public service unions not to use the threat of sanctions to secure a privileged position for themselves at the expense of other groups of workers. It also means that a particularly strong case can be made that public sector unions should submit their claims to arbitration in the event of inability to reach agreement. Strike action against public authorities needs specific justification in terms of substantiated grievance, especially in periods when the Government is seeking to give effect to a policy of voluntary wage restraint. It might, for example, be justified if that policy had a built-in discrimination against public sector workers, or if the authorities had deliberately held back, or drawn out, negotiations to ensure that major claims were caught in the wage-restraint or wage-freeze net – situations which public sector unions have experienced in the past.

In discussing the justification for economic strike action directed against the Government, it is important again to stress the distinction between protest strikes designed to draw the Government's attention to the strength of feeling that exists, and coercive strikes designed to force the Government's hand. To be coercive a strike must be more than a mere inconvenience that can be put up with even for a long period. It must impose a substantial burden or cost which the Government will feel under an urgent obligation to remove as soon as possible. It is clear, therefore, that unions vary greatly in their ability to mount a coercive strike against the Government, as well as in their readiness to do so. Unions are unlikely to challenge the Government unless (a) they have failed to achieve their objectives through negotiation and (b) they believe they are in a strong position to secure their demands or extract major concessions. No union will lightly 'take on' the Government and any union doing so will feel required to justify its challenge. The Government thus invariably finds itself faced not with a precipitate strike, but with the *threat* of strike action in support of clearly defined demands. The threat itself will assume different forms according to the ability of the specific groups of union members concerned to take strike action that would seriously disrupt (a) the working of the machinery of Government, (b) the lives of wide or vulnerable sections of the public, and (c) the working or condition of the economy as a whole.

The Government's attitude to such threats will turn on four factors:

1. Its assessment of the seriousness of the threat in terms of:
(a) the ability of the union to mount and sustain a major stoppage;
(b) the ability of the Government to take counter measures to reduce the disturbance to manageable proportions.
2. The financial and political cost, both immediate and consequential, of meeting the union's minimum demands or providing minimum concessions necessary for a negotiated settlement.
3. The extent to which the Government is committed *in principle* to:
(a) its existing policies and position;
(b) *not* giving in to threats of strike action.
4. The possibility of 'heading off' or delaying strike action by offering to submit the dispute to some independent investigating body.

It is apparent that the chances of union success will be strongest when the 'cost' of making concessions, as seen by the Government, is appreciably less than the 'cost' of facing a protracted strike on an issue to which it is not strongly opposed in principle. Thus there was a much greater chance in 1919 of the miners extracting at strike-point the promise of legislation to reduce the hours of working, than of securing their demand for the nationalization of the mines. No Government could have secured nationalization legislation from a Conservative-dominated House of Commons. Indeed many would go further and question whether, in the early wake of a general election which had overwhelmingly returned candidates of parties opposed to nationalization, the Miners' Federation was justified in threatening coercive strike action to secure what was an essentially political demand. If a case is to be mounted in terms which do not challenge the authority of the Government to govern, it would have to be on the basis that successive Governments had increasingly found it necessary to regulate conditions in the coal industry and that what was then at stake was the return of this strike-torn industry from Government to private control – a reversion which threatened the interests and livelihood of over a million miners.

From the above discussion one might perhaps draw the general conclusion that a trade union is entitled to threaten coercive economic industrial action against the Government only if:

1. It is acting in pursuance of an ordinary trade union objective (which of course would include strikes against Government action which threatened members' jobs).
2. The granting of the union's demands would not be incompatible with the maintenance of the Government's political authority and credibility, unless the Government can reasonably be held directly responsible for the crisis the union faces.
3. The dispute will be conducted in such a fashion as not to cause deep and serious harm to vulnerable sections of the population.

The case for union action will be further strengthened if:
4. The union states its willingness to withdraw its strike threat in return for an independent inquiry, whose findings the Government pledges itself to accept.
5. If any claim to be a special case deserving to be treated as an exception (e.g. in relation to wages policy), has the support of other unions who might otherwise make the same kind of claim on their own behalf.

POLITICAL STRIKES AGAINST THE GOVERNMENT

Coercive strikes in support of strictly political demands can only be assessed in the context of the political system and political situation in which they occur, and the purpose for which they are called. If one is dealing with a highly repressive or autocratic regime it is not difficult, in terms of democratic theory, to justify the use of the strike weapon to secure the overthrow of the Government or major changes in the constitution. It was the widespread strikes in Russia in October 1905 which led the frightened Czar to issue his manifesto promising a constitution, civil liberties and universal suffrage. Conversely democratic theory would condemn strikes, or the threat of strikes, designed to prevent the granting of basic political or human rights to underprivileged or deprived sections of the population, e.g. the threat of strike action by white trade unions in South Africa against the Government's proposals to lift restrictions on blacks working in many fields of employment. The issue is rather different if one is dealing with a strike, not against an authoritarian or inherently repressive regime, but against a constitutional State which refuses to grant basic rights to all its working-class citizens. Thus the Belgian trade unions called general strikes in 1893, 1902 and 1913 in support of the demand for universal manhood suffrage. The use of the strike weapon to secure the right to vote seems fully justified where, as in Belgium in 1893, the authorities stubbornly refuse to grant universal suffrage and fail to agree on any measures to reform and extend the very narrow franchise then existing. The decision to call the Belgian General Strike of 1893 was also justified by events, since within five days the Assembly agreed to a scheme which increased the number of voters tenfold. The strike of 1902, on the other hand, was ill-timed and failed, while that of 1913 was probably unnecessary.[14]

If one turns to the modern democratic State based on universal suffrage the only valid grounds in democratic theory for coercive political strike action that could be made would be that such action was essential to preserve the democratic State itself against (a) internal subversion, (b) Government subversion of democracy, or (c) the catastrophic effects of a morally indefensible

14. E. H. Kossman, 'The Low Countries 1780–1940', *Oxford History of Modern Europe*, Clarendon Press, Oxford, 1978, Ch. VI. 1 and Ch. VIII. 3.

Government policy. Whether any case can be made will, of course, depend on the particulars. The following examples may serve to illustrate the kind of considerations involved.

1. *Saving the democratic State from internal subversion.* In 1920 a successful monarchist-military *Putsch*, lead by Dr Kapp against the new democratic Weimar Republic, was defeated by the combination of the refusal of collaboration by higher civil servants and a highly successful general strike called by the Social Democratic Party.

2. *Saving democracy from Government subversion.* Following the Nazi victory at the polls in 1933, and the attacks on democratic rights which followed on the burning of the Reichstag, a Government decree was issued providing severe penalties against anyone seeking to provoke a general strike. It is just conceivable that a strike then called jointly by the Social Democrats and Communists might have forced the Nazis from office.

3. *Saving the community from the catastrophic effects of a morally indefensible Government policy.* In August 1920 the Labour Party and the T.U.C. set up a National Council of Action pledged to call a general strike if the Government sent troops or munitions to aid the Poles in the war against Soviet Russia which the Poles had initiated.

The third example is the one most open to dispute, but as I have argued elsewhere, given the past record of military intervention against Soviet Russia, the British Labour Movement had strong grounds for believing that the Government would only be deterred from embarking on further intervention to secure the overthrow of the Bolshevik regime by the threat of industrial action.[15] The validity of taking strike action in this case turns on whether, and if so in what terms, one can establish that one's own government is preparing to embark on an unjust war which ought to be resisted.[16] Even if such a case can be established the question still

15. See my article 'Hands Off Russia – British Labour and the Russo-Polish War, 1920', *Past and Present*, December 1967.

16. This is the subject of Michael Walzer's thoughtful book, *Just and Unjust Wars: A Moral Argument with Historical Illustrations*, Allen Lane, 1978.

remains whether there is sufficient support amongst union members to justify issuing a strike call. While both the British attack on Egypt over Suez and the United States war in Vietnam are strong candidates for moral condemnation, in neither case was industrial action contemplated because union members were very far from united in strongly opposing these military adventures. Similarly, while adequate grounds might be adduced for saying that strike action against McCarthyism would have been justified in the early fifties to protect the democratic rights of American citizens, there was a marked absence of condemnation, indeed a marked degree of support for McCarthyism among trade unionists in the United States. There seems no reason, therefore, to expect an excess of commitment to the protection of democratic principles by trade unions through strike action – possibly the reverse.

It is striking that the close association of the trade unions with the Labour Party in Britain has never resulted in any attempt to harness union industrial action to further Labour's political demands or policies. This reflects the constitutional character of both the Labour Party and the trade unions, made possible by the development of the parliamentary democratic system. But, while the Labour Party has consistently adhered to constitutional principles (subject to an implicit recognition that in an extreme emergency coercive political action might be necessary to protect the democratic system itself), there are indications that individual trade unions, or groups of unions, are increasingly prepared to consider undertaking industrial action to force through changes in Government policy in their own immediate area of concern. This may take the form either of seeking to impose a policy on the Government, or more commonly of seeking to prevent the Government giving effect to its declared policies.

A striking illustration is to be found in the dispute over private pay beds in National Health Service hospitals, which had been agreed to by the Labour Government when the Service was set up in 1946. In its election manifesto of October 1974 the Labour Party announced that it 'has started its attack on queue-jumping by increasing the charges for private pay beds in NHS hospitals and is now working out a scheme for phasing private beds out of these hospitals'.[17] In March 1975 the Conference of the Confederation of Health Service Employees (C.O.H.S.E.) threatened the Labour Government with industrial action in the hospitals unless a clear time-table for phasing out pay beds was drawn up by early May. The Government quickly responded by putting up private bed charges by nearly fifty per cent and by announcing that 400 pay beds would be axed by July. It followed this up in August with proposals to abolish all 4,000 remaining private pay beds in NHS hospitals, but providing for new licensing laws for private nursing homes which would permit a comparable increase in the number of acute-case beds in the private sector to offset those to be lost in the NHS hospitals. The National and Local Government Officers Union in September announced its opposition to all private practice and advised its branches how to thwart planning applications for the building of private hospitals. For their part hospital consultants in various hospitals up and down the country decided to treat only emergency cases in order to put pressure on the Government to amend its proposals. In October the Conservative spokesman in the Commons urged doctors to stop this disruptive action, while promising that the Conservatives would restore private beds when returned to office. In January 1976 the British Medical Association balloted hospital consultants on a compromise plan which provided for the early elimination of 1,000 beds; but for the creation of a board representing doctors and other health service staff to supervise the phasing out of the remaining 3,000 beds, without time limit, and in step with the reasonable availability of alternative facilities for private hospital practice. This proposal was accepted by the consultants.[18] The Government's compromise proposals, with some minor amendments made by the Lords, became law in October 1976, and steps were gradually taken to implement them. In May 1979, however,

17. F. W. S. Craig, *British General Election Manifestos 1900–1974*, Macmillan, 1975, p. 460.
18. *The Annual Register*, 1975 and 1976.

the Conservatives won the general election on a programme which included a promise 'to allow pay beds to be provided [in NHS hospitals], where there is a demand for them and end Labour's vendetta against the private health sector and restore tax relief on employer/employee medical insurance schemes'.[19] Within a few weeks C.O.H.S.E. was threatening industrial action and the annual conference of the National Union of Public Employees (N.U.P.E.), in face of executive opposition, passed a resolution instructing 'all N.U.P.E. members to provide no further services to private patients' if the Government had not set a firm date for the removal of all remaining private beds by 1 January 1980.[20]

The issue of private pay beds in NHS hospitals is without question a major political issue on which the two main parties sharply differ. It is also an issue on which there is a sharp division of opinion on the principle of private medicine between the unions representing hospital workers and the professional bodies representing hospital doctors: but with this difference that, whereas the latter have a direct financial interest in maintaining private pay beds, the former has no direct interest in getting them removed. I have already argued that members of the medical profession are *never* entitled to engage in industrial action (pp.138–9 above). In this case the action of the consultants was especially open to objection since it was taken by highly paid persons, in the claimed interests of patients and the principles of the medical profession, when in practice the action served to further their own self-interest and sought to frustrate the Government's political programme for the hospital service. While the unwarranted action of the consultants does not constitute a moral justification for union counter-attacks against pay beds (moreover the initial C.O.H.S.E. threats preceded the consultants' action), it will be readily apparent that once doctors cross the crucial line of sacrificing their patients' interests to what lowly-paid union members see as a sordid combination of self-interest and political prejudice, it becomes virtually impossible to persuade such

19. *Conservative Party Election Manifesto*, May 1979 General Election.
20. The *Guardian*, 21 May 1979.

members to themselves refrain from threatening action in support of the opposite political policy on pay beds, based on egalitarian principles.

The unpalatable truth that needs to be asserted is that coercive industrial action against the Government in furtherance of directly political objectives is a danger to the democratic political system. It is dangerous precisely because it constitutes a direct challenge to the right of an elected Government to give effect to its policies, even where there is no question of such policies involving interference with basic union rights or interests, the fundamental rights of citizens or the maintenance of the democratic system itself. This was clearly brought out in the Protestant 1974 Ulster Workers' Council strike. That strike had as its aim the break-up of the 'power-sharing' Executive of Protestants and Catholics, set up after the June 1973 Ulster Assembly Elections, and the forcing of new elections. Such elections, it was confidently expected, would return a majority of Protestants pledged to end power-sharing and the Sunningdale Agreement which had provided for a Council of Ireland, representing the Ulster, Eirean and British Governments, to deal with a limited range of issues of common concern. A combination of good organization, extensive intimidation and a weak response from the British authorities ensured success for the strike and the collapse of the hopeful experiment of power-sharing.[21] As far as the present Conservative Government is concerned there was the possible danger that the N.U.P.E. example might be followed by other unions – the teachers might threaten strikes unless the commitments to abolish compulsory comprehensive education were withdrawn, and the local government officers unless the proposals for facilitating council house sales were dropped. If such a situation had arisen,

21. It must be admitted, however, that the Ulster Workers' Council had substantial grounds for their assertion that the Protestant majority, led by Faulkner, no longer represented Protestant opinion. In the February 1974 General Election in Britain the Faulknerites failed to win a single Ulster seat. The Protestant militants, led by William Craig and the Rev. Ian Paisley, swept the board except in Belfast West which was won by Gerry Fitt, leader of the predominantly Catholic Social Democratic and Labour Party.

or arises in the future, then the issue of severely curbing the right to strike would come to the forefront of the political scene, with the strong possibility of dire consequences for both the unions and the British political system. Only those suffering from romantic illusions or revolutionary pretensions have any cause for viewing such a prospect with equanimity or hope.

Seven

The Right to Strike as a Fundamental Right

In his book, *What are Human Rights?*,[1] Maurice Cranston argues that human rights are a category of moral rights distinguished from other moral rights in three ways:

1. Universality – 'the rights of all people at all times and in all situations'. (p. 21)
2. Paramountcy – 'A human right is something of which no one may be deprived without a grave affront to justice. There are certain deeds which should never be done, certain freedoms which should never be invaded, some things which are supremely sacred.' (p. 68)
3. Practicality – Human rights are readily transformable into positive rights through legislation, enforced by an international court with real powers.

It is on the basis of these three tests that Cranston concludes that the economic and social rights of the U.N. Declaration of Human Rights are rights of 'a different logical category' whose inclusion 'hinders the effective protection of what are correctly seen as human rights' (p. 65). Economic and social rights are not universal rights since they impose no universal obligations: rather they are universal ideals or aspirations, though they may attain

1. Maurice Cranston, *What are Human Rights?*, The Bodley Head, 1973. The book includes as appendices the texts of the Universal Declaration of Human Rights, the International Covenants on Economic, Social and Cultural Rights and on Civil and Political Rights. All quotations from these documents come from this source.

the status of moral rights for some men as members of particular political communities (p. 69).

Cranston, himself, seems to be in two minds as to whether the right to form trade unions, and with it the right to strike, should be regarded as a 'traditional political right', along with the right to freedom of expression and assembly (p. 62), or as a special economic and social right of employees which 'should not be confused with the common rights of all men' (p. 74). Nevertheless Cranston's approach provides a useful kicking-off point for an analysis of the right to strike as a fundamental human right.

The right to strike does not appear in the 1948 Universal Declaration of Human Rights proclaimed by the United Nations, though article 23(4) states that 'everyone has a right to form and join trade unions for the protection of their interests'. In 1966, however, the General Assembly approved the International Covenants on Economic, Social and Cultural Rights and on Civil and Political Rights which came into force in 1976 after ratification by thirty-five member States. A Human Rights Committee has been established to which a member State, but not an individual, may submit complaints about abuses of civil and political rights by another State party to the Covenant. No provisions for implementation are made with respect to economic, social and cultural rights. Under Article 8.1d of the Economic, Social and Cultural Rights Covenant member States undertake to ensure 'the right to strike, provided that it is exercised in conformity with the laws of the particular country'. This legal proviso appears to severely debase the face-value of the right. One might be led to conclude, for example, that the legal right to strike permitted in England in 1825 met the terms of Article 8.1d, even though the then law (a) prohibited all strikes other than strikes over wages and hours of work, (b) made no provision for peaceful picketing and rendered workers liable for criminal proceedings for 'molesting' and 'obstructing', (c) held workers liable to criminal proceedings for striking in breach of contract. But, it is necessary to read Article 8.1d in the context of the whole Covenant and with special reference to Article 2.2, under which signatories guarantee to exercise Covenant rights 'without discrimination of any kind as to race, colour, sex, language, religion, political or other opinion, national or social origin, property, birth or other status'. In these terms South African laws imposing restrictions on blacks striking, but not whites, are clearly invalid. One might also stress that, not only States forbidding strikes (e.g. Spain under Franco), but States whose law 'does not provide . . . for a collective stoppage of work . . .' are in contravention of the Covenant; especially if, as in Soviet Russia, the trade unions are under the control of the ruling Government Party and kept committed to an anti-strike policy.[2]

It is apparent that the absence of a formal ban on strike action does not in itself guarantee a liberty right to strike, as the suppressed strike at Novocherkaask in the Ukraine demonstrates only too well.[3] The minimum conditions which must be met if the legal right to strike is to be a meaningful right for workers may be

2. The representatives of the Soviet Government at the Committee of Freedom of Association of the International Labour Office in 1955 stated 'Soviet law does not provide, nor has it ever provided, for a collective stoppage of work, where called by workers in support of their demands', quoted by Emily Clark Brown, *Soviet Trade Unions and Labour Relations*, Harvard University Press, Cambridge, Mass., U.S.A., 1966, p. 230

The origin of the present legal position in relation to strikes in Soviet Russia is obscure. Margaret Dewar in *Labour Policy in the USSR 1917–28*, Royal Institute of International Affairs, 1956, quotes from a decree of the People's Commissariat of Labour, 'with the full consent of the Petrograd Metal Workers', dated 19 January 1918, relating to the wages of workers in the Petrograd Engineering Industries, which provided for compulsory arbitration and which concluded 'With the adoption of this decree all strikes, including the "Italian" [sit-downs, go-slows, working to rule] are banned' (p. 165). This decree was used as the model for subsequent agreements in other industries. Margaret Dewar writes 'This strike clause seems to be the only legal basis for the ban on strikes in the USSR, no Government decree ever having been passed on this issue' (p. 28).

3. See Victor Haynes and Olga Semyonova, *Workers Against the Gulag: The New Opposition in the Soviet Union*, Pluto Press, 1979, Section 2, 'The Right to Strike'.

divided into two categories – political conditions and trade union conditions.

Political conditions

1. No Government policy to prevent strikes or break strikes.
2. The great majority of workers have the legal right to strike.
3. Trade unions are:
(a) not controlled by the Government or by the ruling party of a one-party state;
(b) not subjected to police or security service interference or general surveillance.
4. Legal rights of workers and trade unions to:
(a) advocate strike action;
(b) call strike meetings;
(c) appeal for public support for the strikers;
(d) peacefully picket 'struck' premises.
5. Police and security services not under instructions to, or permitted to:
(a) prevent unions and workers taking strike action;
(b) intimidate striking workers or union officials;
(c) stop workers or unions exercising their legal rights;
(d) take no action to prevent others interfering with workers or unions exercising their legal rights.
6. The Government restricts the use of the armed forces in strikes to those occasions when there is no other way of preventing either
(a) a major breakdown in essential supplies and services, or
(b) a major collapse of law and order. In particular the armed services are not used to defeat strikes or intimidate strikers.
7. Government intervention in any strike is directed to bringing about a settlement, not breaking the strike.
8. Trade unions and strikers are not prevented from publicly:
(a) criticizing Government intervention in any dispute;
(b) demanding the withdrawal of troops, police or security services;

(c) calling for public demonstrations of support, including protest strikes by other unions or groups of workers.

9. Strikers, or strike advocators, accused of criminal activities are publicly tried in open court according to the rules of law.
10. Trade unions and workers are not prevented from calling protest demonstrations and strikes against the imprisonment of strikers or union officials.
11. Trade unions and workers are not stopped from campaigning publicly for changes in the law relating to strikes and union rights, and against the way the law is applied by the Government or interpreted by the Courts.

Trade union conditions

1. Independent trade unions, not company unions controlled by the employer.
2. Democratic trade unions with effective provision for:
(a) free election of local officials;
(b) free election of delegates to union conferences with power to determine union policy and amend union rules;
(c) free election by the membership as a whole, or by elected delegates, of the majority of the union's executive committee where
(d) members are not prevented by intimidation or corrupt practices from campaigning for changes in union leadership or policy.
3. Unions with rules and procedures providing for the authorization and calling of strikes – rules and procedures which *are* used for authorizing and calling strikes.
4. Unions with rules and procedures providing for the payment of strike pay – rules and procedures which *are* used to make payments to strikers.

There are a number of articles in the two United Nations Covenants which bear on the political conditions necessary for the right to strike. Thus Article 4 of the Covenant on Economic, Social and Cultural Rights lays down that a State may subject the rights of that Covenant (which includes the right to strike) 'only to such limitations as are determined by law only in so far as this may be compatible with the nature of these rights and solely for the purpose of promoting the general welfare in a democratic society'. This article would lend strong support to most, if not all, the political conditions detailed and especially to 1, 4, 5, 6 and 7. Similar support is provided by Article 5 which lays down that 'Nothing in the present Covenant may be interpreted as implying for any State, group or person any right to engage in any activity or to perform any act aimed at the destruction of any of the rights or freedoms recognized herein, or at their limitation to a greater extent than is provided for in the Covenant.' Article 8.1a guaranteeing 'The right of everyone to form trade unions and join the trade union of his choice . . .' rules out Government or Party controlled trade unions (Political condition 3a); especially if, as normally happens in such cases, no other trade unions are permitted or allowed to exist. Political conditions 8, 10 and 11 are less securely supported by Articles 19 and 21 of the Covenant on Civil and Political Rights. The former states that 'Everyone shall have the right to freedom of expression . . .' and the latter 'The right of peaceful assembly shall be recognized'; in both cases subject to the proviso that the rights may be restricted by law (and only by law), where necessary for the protection of national security, public order, public health, morals, or the rights and freedoms of others. Articles 9, 14 and 15 on the right to a fair trial accord with political condition 9. Although Article 5 of this Covenant repeats the terms of Article 5 of the Economic, Social and Cultural Covenant, there is no equivalent of Article 4, leaving Articles 19 and 21 more open to Government malinterpretation and manipulation than one would wish. Nevertheless the whole thrust of the two Covenants lends powerful support for the minimum political conditions set out above. The failure of any State to meet these minimum conditions is evidence not only that no effective right to strike exists, but that the State concerned is in breach of other major human rights.

The trade union conditions, on the other hand, do not in themselves directly raise, or arise out of, considerations of human rights; except possibly insofar as Article 8.1a would be infringed if employers compelled workers to join company unions, or 'yellow' unions as they are often called. Company unions are no longer of major significance in Western Europe or North America, although they were used in the past to stop the emergence of independent trade unions committed to using the strike weapon to secure their demands. Conditions 3 and 4 are met by ensuring that workers who wish, are not prevented from, or given no opportunity to, join independent trade unions; since the great majority of such unions will of their own accord make provision for calling strikes and making strike pay. If there are no unions with strike powers available for most or all workers, or if such powers are never used or seriously threatened, then this is clear evidence, not simply that independent trade unions; since the great majority of such unions existing. A country whose unions never call strikes is a country where no right to strike exists.

The conditions that unions should be democratic are not strictly necessary for effective strike action; since undemocratically-run unions, like the Teamsters Union in the United States or the Electrical Trades Union in Britain when under Communist control, are not only capable of strike action but do make use of the strike weapon. Democratic control is necessary, however, to ensure that the strike weapon is used on behalf of and when required by the members, and not when it suits the interests of those who control the union. More fundamentally trade unions controlled by criminal or political bosses lack any basis of legitimate authority, and without such authority it is difficult to sustain the claim that the necessary political conditions for strike action must be secured to them by the political authorities. Corrupt leaders, of course, are unlikely to press such claims. It is important to stress, however, that the onus is on the authorities concerned to show that:

(a) the degree and form of criminal corruption or political

manipulation is on such a scale, and so general, that the rights of all unions should be restricted;

(b) the restrictions imposed do not prevent legitimate unions exercising their legitimate functions, including the calling of strikes in support of their demands:

(c) action is taken to facilitate the return of the corrupted or manipulated unions to legitimacy with a view to lifting all restrictions.

Finally nothing in the illegitimate and degenerate character of trade unions in any country can ever be an excuse for depriving workers of their right as workers to take strike action. It is crucial to establish the right to strike as the right of workers *as* workers and not just as union members – a point on which the United Nations Covenant is silent. As a fundamental right the right to strike must be not only a right of workers in the absence of trade unions but a right in the face of union lethargy or hostility, or, in the last resort, a right *against* trade unions.

The recognition that the right to strike may, in certain circumstances, turn into a right against trade unions, strongly suggests that one needs to examine carefully and critically its claims to be accorded the status of a fundamental human right. This can be done by listing and scrutinizing the most distinctive and controversial features of the right to strike which have been revealed in the course of this study. These features may be grouped together under the following headings:

The right to strike as
1. a class right
2. an instrumental right
3. a collective right
4. a coercive right
5. a political right

The Right to Strike

1. A Class right

The right to strike is the right to collectively withdraw one's labour from the person or body to whom it has been contracted. Such categories of *non*-employed persons as employers, partners, self-employed, unemployed, pensioners, students and housewives cannot have a right to strike since they have nobody from whom they may collectively withdraw their labour.[4] They are inherently incapable of striking because of the nature of their economic role and position in society. The right to strike is thus not a universal right of all men but the exclusive right of the economic category of persons who work for others – the working class. More significantly it is a right of that class against another class – the employing class – a feature which it shares with other worker rights provided for in the United Nations Declaration and the Economic Covenant (e.g. the right to a fair wage, and to safe and healthy working conditions). The incorporation of such rights is a recognition not simply that a fundamental conflict of interest is inherent in the employment relationship but that it is the interests of workers not those of employers that deserve and require protection. Although these rights were only established through working-class struggle in the face of strong opposition from employers, and against the prevailing orthodoxy of freedom of contract, they have their origin in, and derive much of their initial force from, traditional conceptions of economic justice – just wages, fair prices and good masters. Trade unions armed with the strike weapon were instruments whereby the working class might wrest for themselves the justice which bad economic masters denied them and misguided political masters refused to secure for them.

The traditional conception of the right to strike as the moral

4. The term 'strike' has been appropriated by other groups of persons for other purposes – thus we hear of rent strikes. But the collective withholding of rents, whether by students or council tenants, is quite distinct from the collective withdrawal of labour, though it too may be used as a weapon or ploy in a bargaining process.

right of good workers against bad employers is in sharp contrast with the radical conception of the right to strike as a class right of workers against employers to further their class interests at the latter's expense, and still more with the Marxist conception which sees strikes as 'the school of war of the workers in which they prepare themselves for the great struggle which cannot be avoided' – 'the decisive battle between bourgeoisie and proletariat'.[5] All three conceptions are to be found within the British trade union movement. The first conception, which finds its most powerful and complete expression in natural justice, is the one easiest to defend in traditional moral terms. Its acceptance would tend to limit the use of the strike weapon to substantiated instances of exploitation or injustice which fell outside the established norms of employer behaviour. In contrast the second conception justifies the use of the strike weapon against employers to raise the general level of all workers, at the expense of all employers and not just of a minority of bad employers. But it stands in need of some moral underpinning, since it is not self-evident that a right to act to secure one's own advantage at the expense of another (whether employer, government or public) has any claim to be accepted as a moral right. The doubtful nature of the assertion is enhanced when we note that, in contrast to other basic human rights, a strong case can be made for prohibiting certain groups of workers from having the right and restricting its use by others. Further, it is accepted as quite legitimate, even laudable, that groups of workers should, either for a limited period or permanently, be permitted to 'trade in' their right to strike in return for other benefits, or even sell it outright.[6] In these terms the right to strike appears as a factor in the collective bargaining process, to be used not by reference to considerations

5. Frederick Engels, *The Condition of the Working Class in England in 1844*, quoted in *Marx and the Trade Unions*, edited by A. Lozovsky, Martin Lawrence, 1935, p. 122.

6. Workers may, of course, 'trade off' or sell their right to leisure in return for higher overtime rates but, except in war time, such action is not normally applauded but seen as, at best, an unfortunate necessity for workers with low basic rates.

of justice or fairness, but to those of cost and the chances of success. The strike weapon will benefit not the weak and exploited, but the strong and well established in the vigilant pursuit of self-interest, without regard to the interests of their fellow workers.

The Marxist conception of power struggle seeks to overcome this moral deficiency by subordinating the right to strike to the duty of securing the liberation of the whole working class from the shackles of capitalist class exploitation. As Marx himself wrote in 1866, the trade unions 'must convince the world at large that their efforts, far from being narrow and selfish, aim at the emancipation of the downtrodden millions'.[7] The right to strike thus appears as one weapon in the armoury of the working class, a weapon which loses its moral purpose if it is used solely as a means to secure narrow and selfish economic ends within the wages system, instead of a means for the abolition of that system.

If one accepts the Marxist conception the problem arises of what legitimate place, if any, the right to strike occupies in socialist society. At first sight the answer might appear to be none, since where there is no exploiting employer class extracting surplus value from workers who now receive the full fruits of their labours, the right to strike would be a right exercised by workers either against themselves or against other workers. It is interesting to note that in 1920 Lenin criticized Trotsky for taking up precisely this position. Lenin then insisted that in 'a workers' State *with a bureaucratic twist in it*' (which is what the Soviet State had become in Lenin's view), it was 'theoretically quite wrong' to argue that 'the trade unions have nothing to protect' – 'we ... must use these workers' organizations to protect the workers from their State, and to get them to protect our State'.[8]

7. 'Instructions for Delegates to the Geneva Congress of the International Working Men's Association' 1866 in K. Marx, *The First International and After*, Political Writings Vol. 3, edited and introduced by David Fernbach, Pelican Books, 1974, p. 92.

8. 'The Trade Unions, the Present Situation and Trotsky's Mistakes', speech delivered on 30 December 1920. *Collected Works of Lenin, Vol. 32, December 1920–August 1921*, Moscow, 1965, pp. 24–5.

The Soviet Free Trade Union Association would doubtless concur.

2. *An instrumental right*

The human rights listed in the United Nations Declaration and Covenants may be divided into two main categories – liberty rights and benefit rights. The primary condition for the enjoyment of liberty rights is that governments refrain from interference and prevent others from doing so. This category includes the traditional liberty rights of life, movement, thought, speech, religion and association; as well as the economic and social rights to own property, choose one's work and to strike. Benefit rights, on the other hand, are entitlements to have some basic human needs met or wants satisfied by Governments or through Government action.

But rights may be classified in another way – into those which are ends in themselves (though they may also be means to other ends) and those which are means or instruments for securing ends. Most rights fall into the former category. The most notable of the instrumental rights are the right to strike and the right to vote.

While the right to vote might appear to differ sharply from the right to strike in that, unlike the former, it is a means for securing only one end – the determination of who shall rule – this is too limited a view since that determination is made by electors concerned with securing varied benefits or avoiding multifarious burdens. The right to vote is an integral part of the political system of a particular State and its exercise, in all but the most extraordinary of circumstances, serves the purposes of that system. Citizens are seen as having a civic duty to exercise their right to vote to demonstrate their belief in the validity of the system and to secure the election of a legitimate government, as well as a civic right to choose between contesting parties and candidates – without which choice the right is meaningless. Where criticism is directed is not at the right itself, but at failure or refusal of some political systems to make the exercise of the right meaningful and possible for all members of the community.

While I may reasonably be asked to justify my choice in voting, voting itself requires no justification.

The right to strike is quite different. It is not an integral part of any system of government and is capable of being exercised, albeit often with considerable difficulty and at considerable risk, under most political systems other than totalitarianism. Even where the right to strike is legally recognized and effectively protected, acts of striking are invariably regretted and accepted as at best 'justified in the circumstances'. Strikes are seen as a last resort weapon not only by the Government and the public at large, but by most trade unionists. Those who decide on strike action commonly seek to justify themselves by putting the 'blame' on 'unreasonable' employers who have 'forced' the workers to take strike action in support of their 'legitimate' demands. The use of this moral language of justification strongly suggests that the right to strike only appears as morally respectable in most people's eyes if the strike is presented as a defensive weapon for protecting established rights or as an offensive weapon for securing just deserts. The status of an instrumental right as a fundamental human right will turn, firstly, on the moral nature of the instrument itself and how it is used and, secondly, on the moral ends served and consequences realized. The moral issues raised by the first are discussed below in section 4 (coercive right).

In examining ends and consequences it is important to recognize that even basic liberty rights, like freedom of speech and publication, may be used for immoral purposes or have objectionable consequences. Some of these may be of so serious a character as to justify imposing legal restrictions on, or conditions to, the exercise of the right: others may justify moral condemnation. What they would not justify is the abrogation of the right, or the imposition of restrictions and conditions of such a character as to seriously impair the value or purpose of the right. Liberty rights, like the right to freedom of speech and publication, have to be asserted and maintained against the claims of established opinion not to be offended and of the authorities not to be subjected to unwarranted criticism. Seen in this light the fact that the right to strike is occasionally used to further purposes which are inherently objectionable in moral terms raises no insoluble problems. In some cases it may be justifiable to proscribe strikes for such a purpose, e.g. to prevent the employment of coloured labour: in others to the assertion that striking in such a case is morally reprehensible, e.g. a strike to force a Jehovah's Witness to join the union or lose his job. In neither case is the validity of the right to strike itself in dispute, especially since such strikes are highly exceptional.

More difficult problems are raised by the fact that many strikes have serious adverse effects on the rights of members of the public. While one may reasonably expect people to put up with inconvenience or annoyance as a price that has to be paid if other persons are to be allowed to exercise their rights, it is not reasonable that they should suffer serious threats or injury to their lives or liberties. In the previous chapter I attempted to show how these valid claims might be met by a combination of a legal denial of the right to strike to a small number of specialist workers (i.e. the police) and a legal proscription of certain extended forms of strike action (i.e. secondary picketing), plus a moral recognition that some groups of workers ought to be willing to forgo the right to strike in return for guarantees of fair treatment, or to accept their responsibility to ensure that the injurious effects of strike action are reduced to acceptable levels.

The most serious objection which can be raised against the right to strike as an instrumental human right is that raised by Marx. If the strike is essentially no more than a means of advancing the selfish interests of particular groups of workers, then it lacks any positive moral value. This does not, of course, mean that the right to strike should be denied legal existence; but it would appear to undermine any claim for its acceptance as a basic human right. It is apparent, however, that self-interest is not in itself an absolute bar to securing moral approval as long as two conditions, one negative and one positive, are met. The negative condition is that the pursuance of self-interest should not be at the expense of the valid interests of others: the positive that the self-interest sought should be accepted, either as fair and deserved, or to the general benefit. While one could not expect to substantiate generally acceptable criteria which would enable one to reach agreement on whether the positive conditions could be met in relation to the right to strike, it is open to question whether the typical run-of-the-mill strike in any modern Western capitalist society would meet the basic moral requirements for validation in terms of *any* value system including Marxism. Only working-class fundamentalists, committed to the belief that the exercise of union power for sectional self-interest must always in some mysterious way work to the ultimate benefit of the working class as a whole, would find no great difficulty in discerning moral justification for groups of well-paid workers using the strike weapon in the winter of 1978/79 to extract wage increases well in excess of increases in the cost of living, in flat opposition to the wage policies both of the Labour Government and the Trades Union Congress.[9]

Many union negotiators would make no such moral claims, but would rest their case for self-interested strike action on the realities of the collective bargaining process under capitalism, whose logic requires each party to maximize advantages, having regard only to the power and position of the opposing party and the need to maintain the bargaining process itself. What is held to be relevant in a strike position is not justice but power – where unions differ is in the actual amount of strike power they have and are conscious of having, and in their readiness to use it. But, while the right to strike as the legal right to secure the greatest good for the sectional interest without regard to others, may be fully compatible with the ethics of the market economy, it lacks any claim to be put on a higher moral plane than the employer right to lock-

9. Working-class fundamentalism in many ways resembles its nineteenth-century middle-class counterpart, economic individualism, which too saw a hidden hand (the forces of the market) working to produce the general advantage.

out, with which it is intimately associated in English law. Only if the former can be given a moral dimension can its claim to be a fundamental right be accepted.

3. A collective right

The right to strike, like the associated right to form and join trade unions, is distinctive in that it can only be exercised collectively. All other fundamental rights are either purely individual rights or rights naturally extendable from individuals as individuals to individuals as members of a group (as with the right to private and to public worship). But what is more significant is that, as a collective right, the right to strike necessarily comes into conflict with individual rights. Thus, as we have seen, while the right of individuals to form and join trade unions is not logically incompatible with the right of individual employers to run their businesses in their own way by refusing to employ union labour, in practice it is so. Unionization means the end of the right of workmen and employers to settle pay and conditions between themselves on an individual basis and imposes considerable limitation on the employer right to unilaterally make changes in the running of his business. Such restrictions are now generally accepted as desirable to redress the balance in the work relationship by taking account of the interests of workers as persons with rights in their work and jobs, instead of as objects in, or commodities of, production.

The right to strike, as seen through union eyes, involves the denial of other established employer rights – the right to dismiss strikers, to engage alternative sources of labour, to get non-strikers to do the job of strikers; as well as the reciprocal right of other workers to take the place of strikers, whether on a temporary or permanent basis. What we have here is the logical working out by workers of their requirements in the right to strike so it may effectively serve their collective purposes. The right to strike as the right of workers collectively to withdraw their labour, leaving employers with the right to find or import substitute labour, is of limited value. The right to strike must be a firm and forceful denial by strikers of any moral right of the employers to give *their* jobs to other workers or of other workers to take *their* jobs from them. Such claims, though bitterly contested in the nineteenth and early twentieth centuries, now find broad acceptance in popular morality, if not in law.

Individual rights are much more seriously and questionably affected by the extension of 'closed' or 'union' shop arrangements in Britain which deny the individual the right not to 'be compelled to belong to an association' (Article 20 of the United Nations Universal Declaration of Human Rights), on pain of dismissal. Increasingly workers in Britain are losing their right to join trade unions and instead are being required to do so. The moral case for workers joining trade unions no longer has to be made – membership is bound up with, indeed part of, the employment relationship. Unions are becoming institutionalized as part of the managerial process and externalized in relation to the worker. Workers are, moreover, normally tied under 'closed' or 'union' shop agreements to a specified union – they may not exercise a right of choice as to which union they join or the right to form a trade union, as laid down in Article 8 of the International Covenant on Economic, Social and Cultural Rights. Where workers covered by 'closed' or 'union' shop agreements are not permitted to opt out from union membership on religious or conscience grounds, there is a clear infringement of the right of freedom of thought, conscience and religion (Article 18 of the International Covenant on Civil and Political Rights).

This development has important repercussions for the right to strike, since the proper exercise of that right by a trade union is held to impose a duty on its members to comply. But if membership is obligatory it is not clear in what sense, if any, 'forced-choice' union members could be said to be under a moral obligation to obey a union strike call, because it proceeded from a body authorized to make such decisions. If 'closed' or 'union' shop agreements become established as the norm in Britain, and they are growing rapidly,[10] a position would quickly be reached whereby a majority of union members had never had the basic right to join their unions, and thereby to validate by their choice of membership the right of representative union bodies to impose on them the *duty* to respond to a union strike call. Workers would thereby have been deprived of an important ingredient of the *right* to strike.

It would, however, be wrong to suggest that such a development would, in itself, deprive the right to strike of any meaning for ordinary workers. The vast majority of strikes are not called, or even authorized, by central union authorities, but by workers on the job through the agency of strike meetings. The individual worker's right in such circumstances, however, is not the right to personally decide whether to strike, but the right to participate in reaching a strike decision. Though difficulties may arise and undesirable practices creep in, the strike meeting is an inherently satisfactory way for workers collectively to exercise the right to take strike action. The main defect from the point of view of the minority opposed to strike action is the absence of means for, and strong opposition to the idea of, taking concerted action to campaign for the termination of a dispute once decided upon. Given the nature of the setting in which strike situations arise, and the deep emotions raised in major disputes, it would be unrealistic and unreasonable to expect the rights of anti-strikers to be provided for and accepted. In the context of 'free choice' trade unionism the right to strike has strong claims for acceptance as a democratic collective right.

10. Moira Hart, 'Why bosses love the closed shop', *New Society*, 15 February 1979, shows that the number of non-managerial workers in manufacturing industry employed in closed shops has increased by nearly a half since the early sixties to 37 per cent for manual and non-manual workers, and to 46 per cent for manual workers alone.

4. A coercive right

Perhaps the most structurally distinctive and morally doubtful feature of the right to strike is its coercive nature. No other human right exists for the purpose of forcing others to do what they do not want to do. The right to strike is the right to threaten action consciously designed to cause harm or injury to persons engaged in the lawful and peaceful pursuit of their own interests. Moreover, while the right to strike is a class right of workers in their struggles against employers, its collective character often requires, or involves, the use of varying degrees of coercion against individual workers. The right to strike is seen by trade unionists, though not by the law, as the right to *require* fellow workers to comply with a strike decision, as well as a right to prevent other workers taking over their jobs.

The justification for the existence of a right of workers to take coercive action against their employers is to be found in the unequal and authoritarian nature of the employment relationship. Workers must be free to organize if they are to have any chance of bargaining on anything like equal terms with their employer and to bargain effectively they need sanctions. As Kahn-Freund and Bob Hepple have written, 'If the workers are not free by concerted action to withdraw their labour, their organizations do not wield a credible social force. The power to withdraw their labour is for the workers what for management is its power to shut down production, to switch it to different purposes, to transfer it to different places.'[11] It might appear, however, that with the extension of collective bargaining to cover virtually the whole industrial field, and with the great increase in Government control of industry, exclusive managerial prerogatives have already been considerably eroded, and with this erosion part of the case for the pre-eminent position of the right to strike. Moreover in recent years employers have virtually ceased to proclaim or to use their legal rights of lock-out and replacing strike labour. They do not take

11. O. Kahn-Freund and Bob Hepple, *Laws Against Strikes*, Fabian Society, 1972, p. 8.

the initiative in labour conflict or seek to wage industrial war. While these developments in no way imply that workers no longer have any need for a legal right to strike, it does suggest that the moral case for taking strike action will in most cases be weaker than it was forty or more years ago. It may be, of course, that many morally justified strikes were not then called because of the relative weakness of the workers and their organizations; but it would appear from the very high proportion of current strikes which are unofficial and unconstitutional that many strikes are not called as a 'last resort'. Moreover it is apparent that increasing use is being made of what has been called 'cut-price' industrial action – overtime bans, work-to-rules, as well as 'lightning' strikes of less than one day's duration, especially in plants with full-time shop stewards.[12] Workers are learning to select the most suitable and economical tool for securing a specific objective. Far from collective bargaining appearing as an alternative to strike action, as it did to many nineteenth-century union leaders, industrial action and the threat of industrial action have become a constituent element of the collective bargaining process. Consequently, the growth of collective bargaining, especially at workshop and plant level, has been associated, not with any withering away of the strike, but rather with the flowering of all forms of industrial action.

But if the right to strike has in large part ceased to be what it was in the nineteenth century, the only effective means available for workers to use against the countervailing power of a hostile employing class to secure a measure of economic justice, then it would seem to lack the distinctive qualities which would entitle it to be designated as a basic human right. Why should it be elevated above the other worker rights to 'go slow', to ban overtime, to work to rule, or even above employer rights to lock-out, delay negotiations and threaten lay-offs?

12. Information from a study of workshop industrial relations in British manufacturing industry carried out by I.F.F. Research Ltd on behalf of Warwick University Industrial Relations Research Unit, quoted in the *Sunday Times*, 12 November 1978.

The Right to Strike

The right to strike is also vulnerable to criticism as a right used to coerce other workers, though it should be noted that such coercion is not a necessary consequence of strike action. It will not arise where:

1. all workers support strike action;
2. all workers are prepared to abide by a strike decision (by strike meeting or authoritative union body);
3. strikers recognize the right of non-strikers to continue working;
4. strikers are not strong enough to exercise coercion against non-strikers.

Few strikers, however, are likely to accept the moral right of non-strikers to exercise their legal right to continue working, and in few cases are the strikers likely to be so weak that they are unable to mount some form of pressure on 'blacklegs'. The more bitter and serious the issue in dispute, the greater the resentment which will be felt against those who refuse to join in — resentment which will always appear as hostile and menacing and which is liable to assume the shape of intimidation or molestation. Such coercion is natural in situations where strike failure is likely to result in strikers losing their jobs or being otherwise victimized. It is much less defensible under conditions where strikers do not put their jobs and positions at risk, where the number of non-strikers is small, and where the issues at stake are not of fundamental importance. These conditions are much more common today than they were in the past and there is consequently less reason to excuse coercive action, especially where it goes beyond the limits laid down by law.

Since the right to strike has always been seen and applied by strikers as the right to force non-strikers to quit work, its status as a basic right appears doubtful, especially since no moral case has ever been made, or perhaps could be made, for imposing on workers a legal duty to strike. But even if one were to accept that workers ought to be legally required to strike, this acceptance would not imply, in the absence of legal compulsion, that strikers themselves were entitled to exercise the compulsive powers the law ought to possess.

It might be argued that much of the discussion about the coercion of individual workers in a strike situation is misconceived, since it ignores the fact that where men decide collectively to exercise a right each binds himself to abide by the collective or representative determination instead of his own individual will. As far as human rights are concerned, however, the most fundamental of them are inalienable. No man may either divest himself, or permit others to divest him, of his right to freedom from slavery, recognition as a person, or a fair trial. In the case of other rights it is held acceptable that persons should be able to bind themselves as members of a particular body not to exercise a right. Thus Catholic priests bind themselves not to marry and Jehovah Witnesses not to vote. In each case the renunciation of rights is self-assumed and relinquishable, since the individuals concerned may, if they wish, defy the ban and risk expulsion, or quit. It is precisely because no such retreats are available (or only at very heavy cost) that one cannot accept that organizations whose membership is compulsory are entitled to impose rules or conditions which deny, or seriously restrict, the basic human rights of its members. That principle is, as we have seen, embodied in the United Nations Declaration of Human Rights requirement that 'no one may be compelled to belong to an association' (Article 20.2).

Whereas with most human rights there is either no strong or meaningful sense in which the negative form of the right can be urged or exercised (i.e. the right to a fair trial), or no sharp conflict between a positive and a negative exercise of the right (i.e. the right to vote), with the right to strike there is an in-built possibility of conflict.[13] This is because it is only with the exercise

13. The only other human rights in which an inherent conflict appears between positive and negative forms is with the right to live (the right not to live), and the right to work (the right not to work). The former conflict

187

of the right to strike that the possibility emerges of exercising the right not to strike. Moreover, the positive exercise is a collective one, not only in that it has to be carried out by a number of workers acting together, whereas the negative exercise is carried out by workers as individuals; but also in the deeper sense that it is carried out in the name of, and on behalf of, a whole group of workers *including* the individuals wishing to exercise their right not to strike. Strikers collectively feel impelled to dissuade individuals who wish to exercise their right not to strike from doing so, since such rights acts appear as acts of individual self-interest which both challenge the authority of the collectivity and undermine the collective effort and purpose.

The accepted legitimate sources of authority for taking strike action are official union bodies and strike meetings, each of which claims the right to bind workers to comply with strike decisions, and to apply sanctions against those who refuse or fail to do so. Figure 5(a) shows diagramatically concentric rings of workers against whom a striking trade union may claim the right to exercise coercion. It will be readily apparent that it is only against those in the innermost ring (ii) 'free-choice' union members, that a direct and unquestionable claim can be made for conformity with the strike decision. 'Forced-choice' members (iii) might reasonably argue that compulsion relieves them of any moral obligation to comply deriving from the mere fact of membership, as distinct from any deriving from the nature or purpose of the strike itself. However, as union members, such persons are in no position to assert, let alone establish, a moral right not to strike, since in trade union thinking they are held to occupy exactly the same moral position as free-choice members. Consequently it is likely that few 'forced-choice' members will themselves see the situation as one in which they have a moral right of choice with regard to compliance with a union strike call, a right they are deprived of by the force of union coercive power. It is in this

---

arises out of irresoluble differences of view as to the nature and meaning of life, while the latter derives from a lack of precision in the social right itself – one needs to establish what is meant by a right to work.

respect that the position of the non-union member (iv) differs from that of the 'forced-choice' union member. The former will see no moral force in a union strike call, nor will the union claim authority over such persons. What it may well claim is that such persons have no right to thwart union purposes by not striking, especially since they stand to benefit from the success of the strike cause. Finally a union may take coercive action (e.g. by secondary picketing) against workers in outside firms who supply goods or services, or who distribute or utilize its products (v), simply on the grounds that such activities lessen the impact of the strike.

It is readily apparent that as one moves outward the claims to

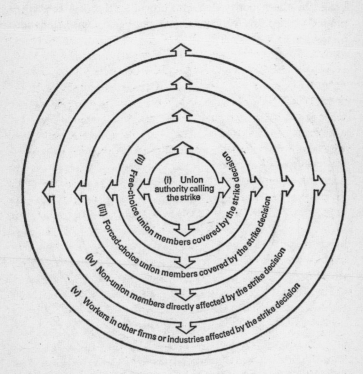

Figure 5(a) Coercive authority – officially called strike

use coercive authority become increasingly contentious and increasingly contested by those against whom coercion is directed. A right to strike as a right to force outside workers to support your strike is of questionable legal validity. As a moral claim it has no possibility of recognition. Further it is impossible to accept that non-union members are without rights in a strike situation. While they may legitimately be subjected to persuasion, denunciation or ostracism, they may not be prevented from working by force, intimidation or threats.

If one turns to the other source of authority for taking strike action, the strike meeting (Figure 5(b)), similar problems arise. It is acceptable that the minority opposing strike action (ii) should be bound by the majority decision, providing that the meeting is properly called and conducted (see pp. 94–7 above). It is also

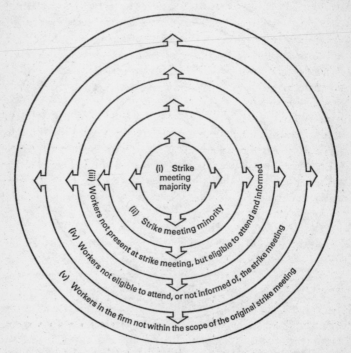

Figure 5(b)   Coercive authority – strike called by strike meeting

The Right to Strike as a Fundamental Right

reasonable to insist that those who knew of the strike meeting and were eligible to attend but did not (iii) are also bound by the strike vote result. Such persons have no moral claim to be exempt from the obligations imposed by the strike decision, unless a case can be made for denying the authority of the strike meeting to meet or to take any decision.

The circumstances are very different when one turns to the position of those unable to attend a strike meeting either because they did not know it was being held, or because they were ineligible to do so, e.g. as non-union members (iv). Provided, however, that reasonable steps were taken to inform eligible persons of the meeting, it is not unreasonable to claim that persons accidentally not informed ought to comply with the decision. Any person ineligible to attend, on the other hand, has no moral obligation to comply and may claim the right to decide for himself whether to personally withdraw his labour alongside those obligated by the strike decision. If he decides to exercise his legal and moral right not to strike he is entitled to do so; although he may legitimately be subject to pressure by strikers, not on the grounds that he had no claim to exercise the right not to strike, but on the grounds that his decision was wrong. Finally there is the complex of problems associated with attempts to extend the scope of a strike to groups of workers not present at, or covered by, the initial strike decision (v) (see pp. 98–105 above). Such persons have no obligations to join the original strike and may not rightfully be subjected to coercive pressure to secure their adherence. The only legitimate way that obligations may be established by such workers is through separate strike meetings.

The fundamental difficulty which emerges is that, especially in bitterly contested disputes, strikers are very liable to seek to extend the area of their claimed authority to include workers in rings (iv) and (v) and to exert coercive, as distinct from persuasive, pressure against such workers to secure their forced adherence to the strike. In consequence workers who might legitimately claim a moral right to exercise their legal right not to strike are prevented from doing so. This clearly has serious consequences for the moral standing of the right to strike as a human right.

5. A political right

Whether human rights exist in any country depends not at all on whether its Government subscribes to the United Nations Declaration of Human Rights, but solely on whether the political system in the country concerned permits and protects the exercise of the rights so universally proclaimed and so extensively trampled on. It is for this reason that the rights of freedom of expression, assembly and association are of such fundamental importance; for unless these exist there can be no public challenge to Government violation of rights. Human rights are always more flagrantly violated where Governments are most effective in suppressing the rights of political expression and organization.

What is true of these rights is also true, if in a less direct sense, of the right to strike. Where no right to strike exists, other human rights too will be found to have a mere paper existence. The reasons are not difficult to discern. The right to strike as an effective right depends, as has been argued above, on the existence of political conditions permitting independent and free trade unions to campaign on behalf of their members and to take strike action, without being subject to police or security force interference or surveillance. Where such conditions are not met the right to strike is either not recognized at all (as in Nazi Germany and Franco Spain), or is a purely nominal right (as in the communist States). In either case it may be possible for workers to mount a strike but at high personal risk, which will vary according to the ruthlessness and determination of the regime concerned. Strikes are particularly anathema to communist States, since they expose in a particularly blatant way the hollowness of their claim to have established socialist societies devoted to the protection and furtherance of the interests of working people. In consequence the prevention of strikes is a major responsibility of trade unions in communist States, and the suppression of information about strikes an important duty of the mass media. Far from the absence or near absence of strikes or public knowledge of strikes being evidence that workers in communist States have no need or desire to strike, since adequate facilities exist for settling disputes in other ways, it is indicative of the absence of basic political rights. Workers in socialist States, as in capitalist States, require a right to strike against managers, union officials and government bureaucrats who fail to protect their legal rights as workers, or who exploit the workers to further their own selfish or corrupt interests.[14] In these narrow terms it might be thought that the withdrawal of the proscription on striking would further rather than undermine the purposes of the communist States. But the right to strike once conceded is not easily circumscribed and Soviet workers might well turn, as their Czarist forebears did, from economic strikes to political strikes directed against the regime. Moreover, economic strikes may spread and assume such a scale as to threaten the authority of the Government, as happened in Poland in 1970 and 1976. The demand for the right to strike, like the demand for free elections, is one which Communist States cannot meet, since it would mean putting into the hands of the working people weapons capable of breaking the monopoly power of the ruling guardian class.

One major difference between the strike weapon and the vote weapon is that the latter, unlike the former, is capable of being transformed into a tool of authoritarian rule. Given the realities of political power in communist States individual voters can readily be persuaded to dutifully record their votes for the only party available for their choice. No such orchestration is possible with the strike. The strike is a collective weapon of attack, and unlike the vote, cannot readily be made to serve the purposes of the political authorities. Strikes have therefore to be prevented, and if this fails, swiftly and quietly suppressed before they spread or get out of hand.

Communist States are not the only States which seek to con-

14. These issues are discussed briefly by Victor Haynes and Olga Semyonova, op. cit.

tain or repress strike activity. Authoritarian regimes of the Right, in Latin America, have done so for decades with considerable success, to the benefit of the indigenous ruling class and of foreign investors.[15] The strike in Latin America performs a similar role to the role it performed in Czarist Russia – as a weapon of the depressed and exploited to improve their lot and to demand political reforms and political rights. In some of the new poor States of black Africa, on the other hand, where the majority still scrape a wretched living from the soil, it has been argued that the organized workers are a relatively privileged and powerful group who ought not to be allowed to press their advantages at the expense of the rural poor by threatening strike action against weak and vulnerable Governments.[16] On these grounds, it is claimed, there is a strong case for the new African States restricting or forbidding trade union strike action.

Expressed in these terms, the case for political restriction of the right to strike appears strong, and points to the critical conclusion that the right to strike is a luxury right which cannot be afforded by poor nations. Such a conclusion appears unwarranted, however, since:

1. the economic gap between urban and rural workers assumes the form of a social gulf between the 'labour aristocracy' and the poor only if the former is restricted to the small group of skilled workers and the latter extended to embrace unskilled and unemployed urban, as well as rural, workers;
2. the economic gap and social gulf between the 'labour aristocracy' and the poor is much less than that between the 'labour aristocracy' and the new middle class of politicians, high civil servants, professional men, business men and managers;
3. industrial action by skilled workers in support of their econ-

15. See, for example, Hobart A. Spalding, Jr. *Organized Labor in Latin America*, New York University Press, 1977.
16. See F. Fanon, *The Wretched of the Earth*, Penguin Books, 1965, Ch. 2, and G. Arrighi and J. Saul in *Essays on the Political Economy of Africa*, Monthly Review Press, 1973.

omic interests need not be, and often is not seen to be, in conflict with the interests of the poor, whether rural or urban;

4. restrictions on strike activity to keep down labour costs operate in many African States to the advantage of the middle classes or foreign investors and not of the urban or rural poor;

5. many African States which prohibit the right to strike pursue policies which accentuate economic inequality and promote the interests of the middle classes, without regard to, or to the disadvantage of, the interests of the urban and rural poor. Other States are grossly corrupt and inefficient. Such States are precluded from claiming entitlement on public interest grounds to restrict the right of trade unions to pursue *their* own sectional interests.

Tanzania is one of the few African States which have pursued egalitarian policies; but even here it is questionable whether the replacement of free trade unions by one Government-controlled union, and the prohibition of strikes, has served to further the realization of the country's socialist objectives. Nyerere himself, in 1971, accepted that strikes against arrogant and unsympathetic managers and bureaucrats were strikes in furtherance of the Government's goals;[17] while the Chairman of the Permanent Labour Tribunal, reporting in 1973 after extensive wage strikes, announced that 'practically in all strikes investigated by us, most of the workers' grievances were found to be true'.[18]

17. The *Nationalist*, 18 November 1971, quoted in 'Socialist Development and the Workers in Tanzania' by M. A. Bienefeld, *The Development of an African Working Class: Studies in Class Formation and Action*, edited by Richard Sandbrook and Robin Cohen, Longmans, 1975, p. 253. Part III of this book, 'Contemporary Working Class Action', is a valuable source of information on the African 'labour aristocracy' thesis. See also Richard Sandbrook's *Proletarians and African Capitalism: The Kenyan Case 1960–1972*, Cambridge University Press, 1975 and Richard Jeffries, *Class, Power and Ideology in Ghana: The Railwaymen of Sekondi*, Cambridge University Press, 1978, Ch. 8, 'Class formation in Ghana'.

18. *Sunday News*, 18 March 1973, quoted in Sandbrook and Cohen, op. cit., p. 256.

The Right to Strike

It is still a historically open question whether it is possible to have a democratic socialist society which respects human rights; but what historical experience does show is that, if such a society is ever to be realized, it will have to be on the basis of free trade unions possessing and exercising the right to strike. Where workers are persuaded to relinquish their weapons in the cause of socialist equality they find, too late, the ugly face of capitalism or colonialism replaced by the faceless mask of the State and party bureaucracy, pierced by the cold hard eyes of the security services.

CONCLUSION

In spite of all the objections that may be raised against accepting the right to strike as a fundamental human right, the political case for doing so is, in my view, an overriding one. Where the legal right to strike is a reality, there one finds free trade unions taking strike action without fear or threat of State interference and repression. It is precisely because strikes are a weapon of mass worker protest that Governments cannot manipulate the right to strike to their own advantage, or neutralize it as they can with the right to vote. It is, therefore, the best barometer we have of the actual condition of democratic and human rights in the various States of the world. But more important still, the distinctive quality of the right to strike as a weapon of working-class struggle means that, not only is it employed to defend established democratic and human rights, but that, except under conditions of extreme political repression, proscriptions on strikes may be defied and a struggle conducted to secure democratic and human rights, as well as economic benefits, from authoritarian governments. The right to strike, like the right to vote, may be misused and, like the right to free speech, may need to be legally restricted to protect the vital interests of others, but it remains one of the great keystones of democratic political society.

Index

Index

Index

More About Penguins
and Pelicans

For further information about books available from
Penguins please write to Dept EP, Penguin Books Ltd,
Harmondsworth, Middlesex UB7 0DA.

In the U.S.A.: For a complete list of books available
from Penguins in the United States write to Dept CS,
Penguin Books, 625 Madison Avenue, New York,
New York 10022.

In Canada: For a complete list of books available from
Penguins in Canada write to Penguin Books Canada Ltd,
2801 John Street, Markham, Ontario L3R 1B4.

In Australia: For a complete list of books available from
Penguins in Australia write to the Marketing Department,
Penguin Books Australia Ltd, P.O. Box 257, Ringwood,
Victoria 3134.

In New Zealand: For a complete list of books available from
Penguins in New Zealand write to the Marketing Department,
Penguin Books (N.Z.) Ltd, P.O. Box 4019, Auckland 10.

Violence for Equality: Inquiries in Political Philosophy

Ted Honderich

Is political violence justifiable?

With force and elegant reasoning, Ted Honderich questions the morality of political violence and challenges the presuppositions, inconsistencies and prejudices of liberal-democratic thinking.

For this volume, the author has revised and greatly enlarged his highly praised *Three Essays on Political Violence*. The five essays which go to make up *Violence for Equality*, given as political philosophy lectures in Britain, Ireland, the United States, Canada, France, Africa and Holland, in fact comprise a completed treatise on the subject.

'Very good, very original . . . enormous merit . . . should be examined and re-examined by anyone interested not only in philosophy, but in the ordinary discourse of politics' – *Listener*

'Clear, rational and continuously interesting' – *New Statesman*

'Inherent interest and importance' – *The Times Higher Education Supplement*

'Masterful argument' – *The Times Literary Supplement*

Arguments for Socialism

Tony Benn

Tony Benn, the most controversial figure in British politics, outlines a strong democratic-socialist approach to the most crucial issues in our political life over the next decade.

'Benn's faith in the capacity of ordinary people to govern themselves emerges here as the most attractive feature of the politics of a man so often caricatured by the popular press as the Labour Party's major threat to democracy and freedom' – David Coats in the *Literary Review*

'Of importance not only to the Labour movement but also to the country as a whole' – Giles Radice in the *Tribune*

'Lively and provocative' – Paul Johnson in the *Sunday Telegraph*

People Power: Community and Work Groups in Action

Tony Gibson

'Our people have no experience of managing for themselves.
They always had the landlord to tell them all his rules; and
at work the boss. Even at school they always had the
teacher telling them what to do.'

Even inexperienced people can be powerful when they act
together. *People Power* is about such groups who, dissatisfied
with the way bureaucrats and managers are running their lives,
have done something about it. It is also a guide for individuals
and groups who may be planning to take action at a local
level.

Part One outlines the strategies of groups who have made
their mark in housing, industry, education and neighbourhood
improvement. The most successful of these groups set out
not to destroy existing structure, but to combine the
knowledge of all their members with the skills of the
professionals.

Part Two contains a Fact Bank which provides basic
technical, legal and financial information, and which will
help groups to get at the facts they need and to handle them
confidently. Using the Fact Bank, groups should be able to
extend their links to the rest of the community and work out
their objectives within the context of local resources.

Use *People Power* to get your action group started!

The Meaning of Conservatism

Roger Scruton

What is a conservative?

Is he a committed capitalist, an upholder of class distinctions, a defender of privilige? Does he have a consistent doctrine, or does he act by instinct, self-interest and laissez-faire?

Roger Scruton challenges those who would regard themselves as conservatives, and their opponents. Locating the system of beliefs that make up the conservative outlook, he argues that these have little in common with the creed of liberalism and are only tenuously related to the doctrine of 'market economy'. The evils of socialism, he maintains, lie precisely where its supporters find its strengths, and he goes on to reject the political vision that has made the conservative position seem outmoded and irrational.

His book presents a new and striking challenge to Marxism, pointing out that the Marxist conceptions can be used to formulate conclusions diametrically opposed to socialist dogmas, and offers new perspectives on the prevailing liberal theories of law, citizenship and the state.